Polish Swear Word Coloring Book

I0481358

By: Shazza T. Jones

Introduction

Learn some Polish swear words while you sit back and colour the pages.

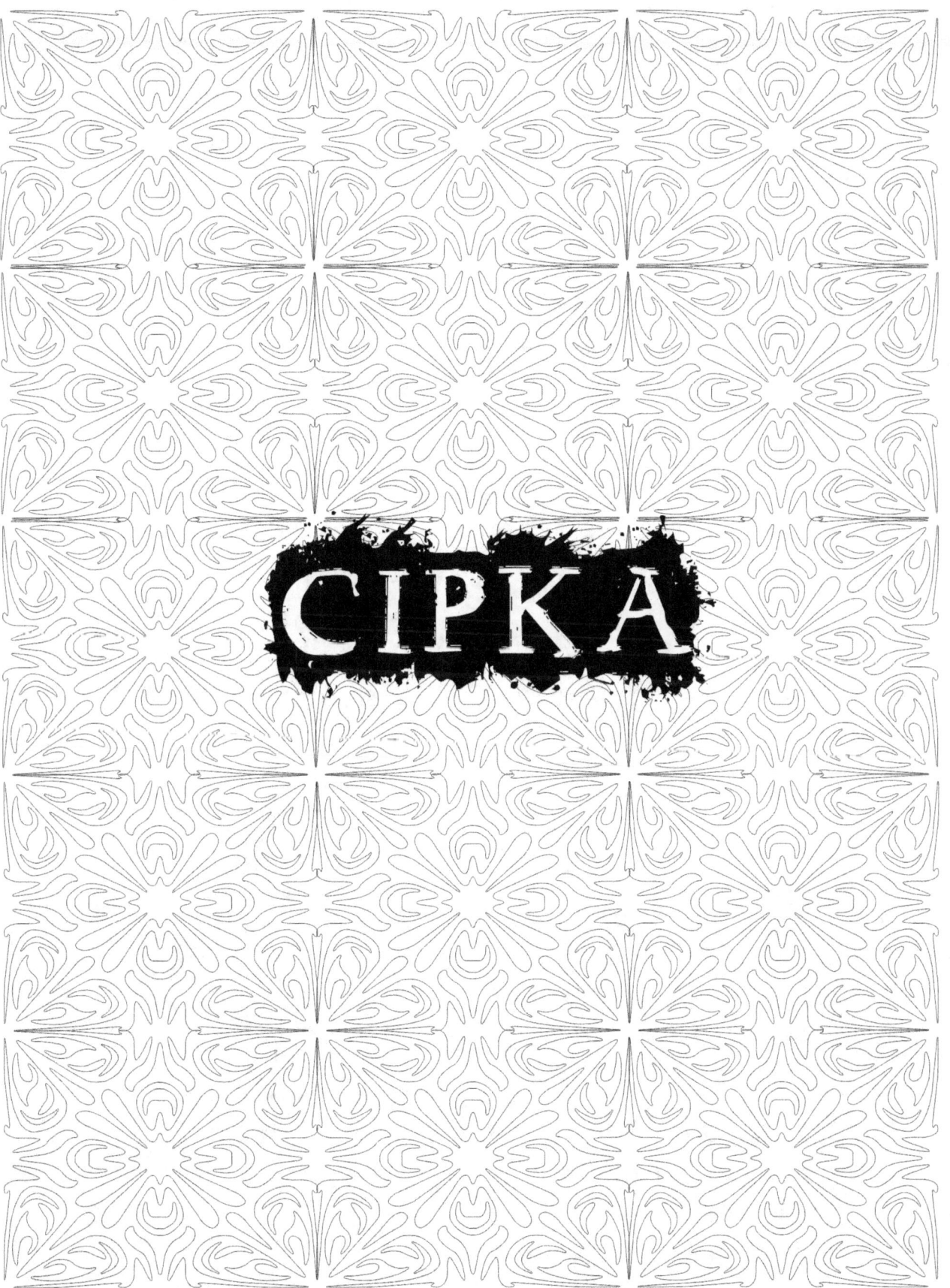

CIPKA

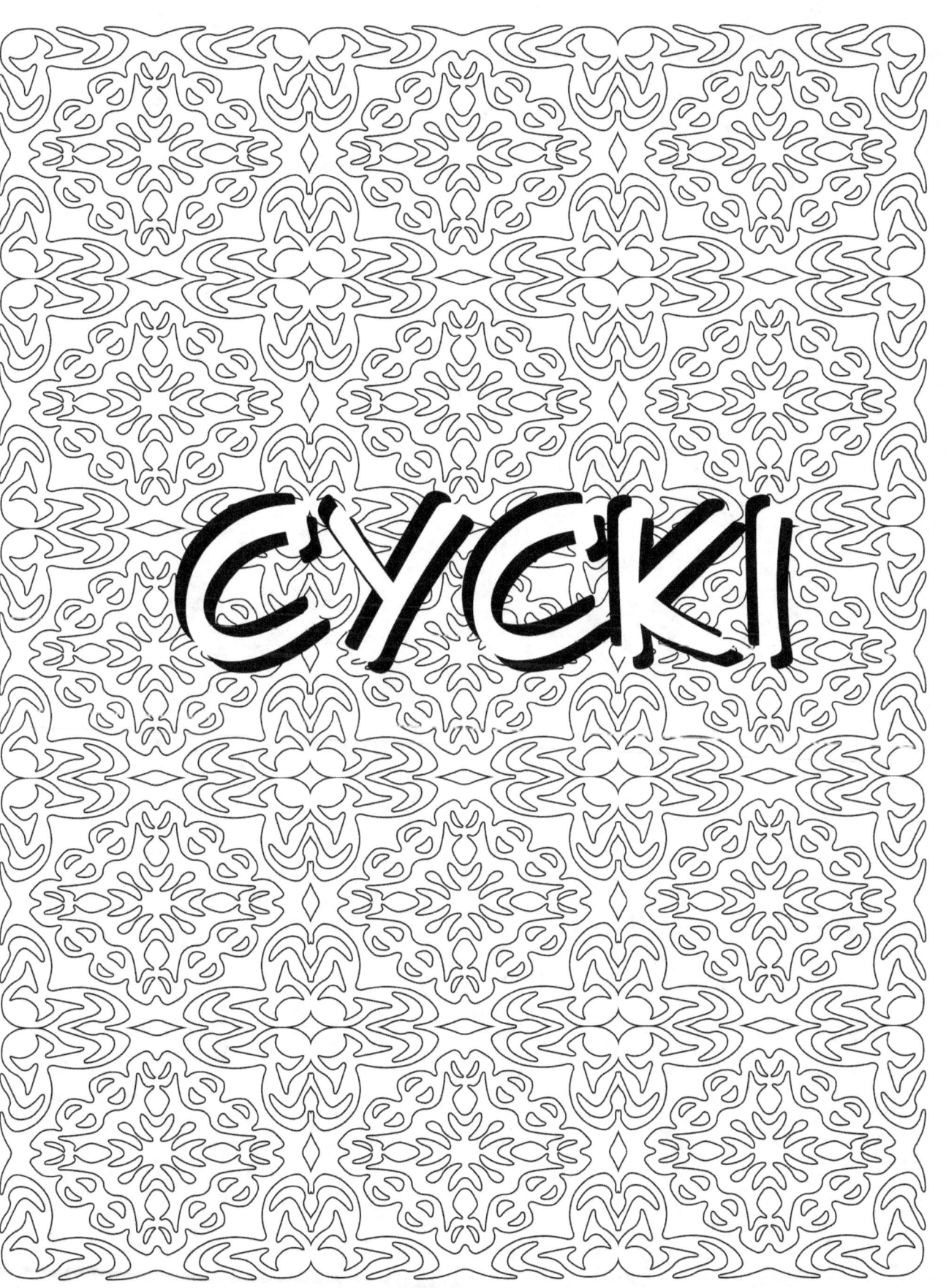

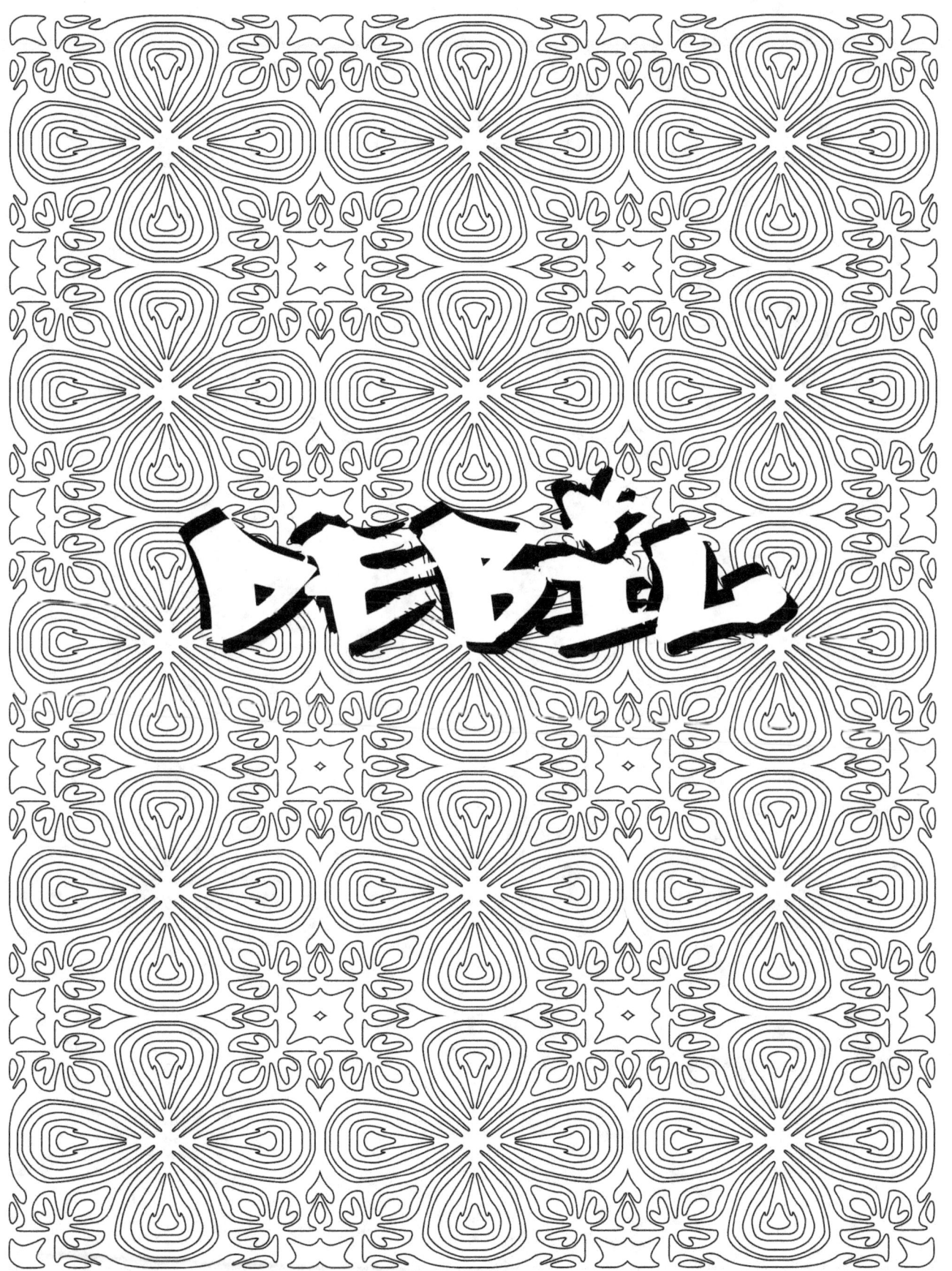

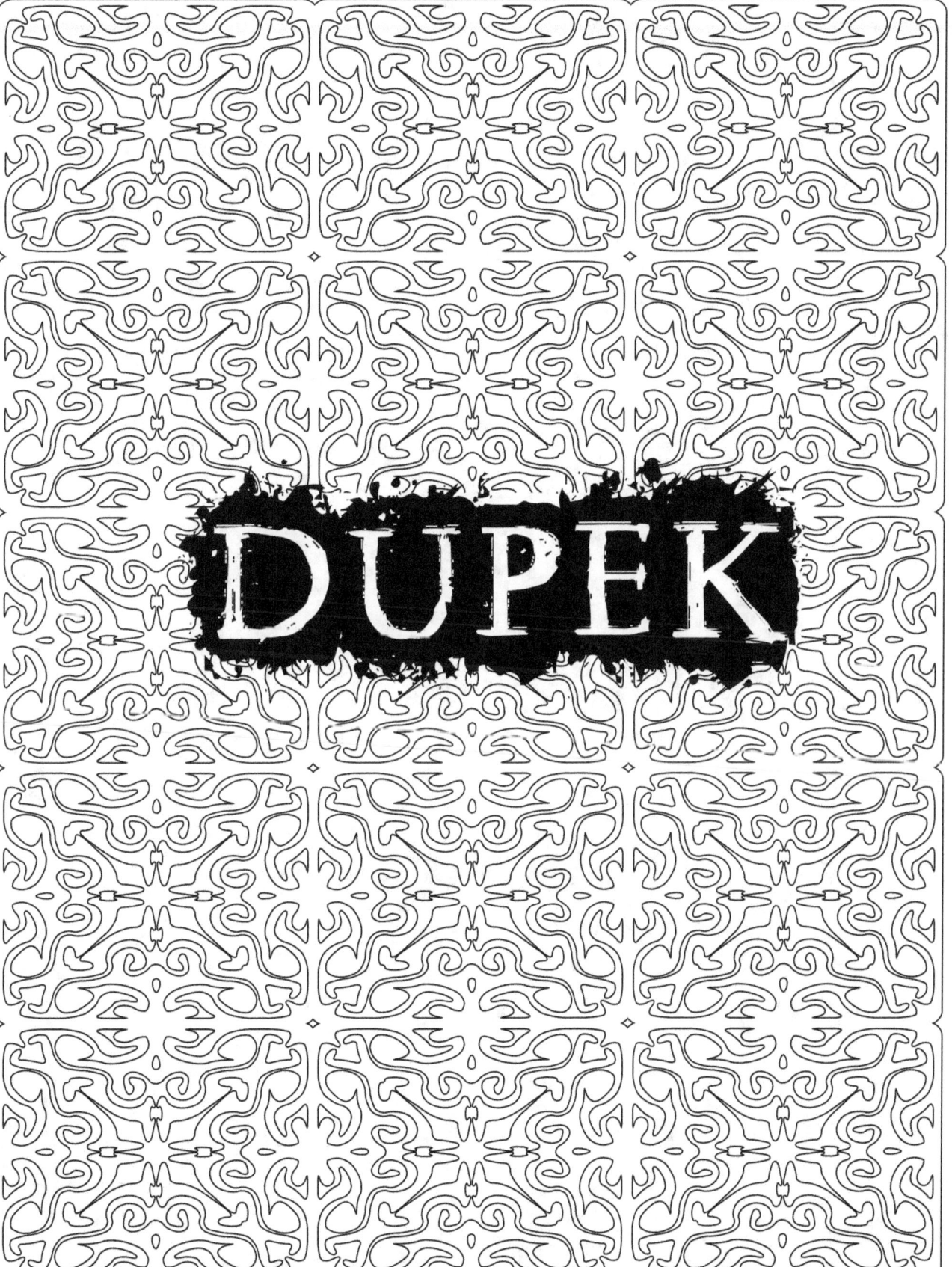

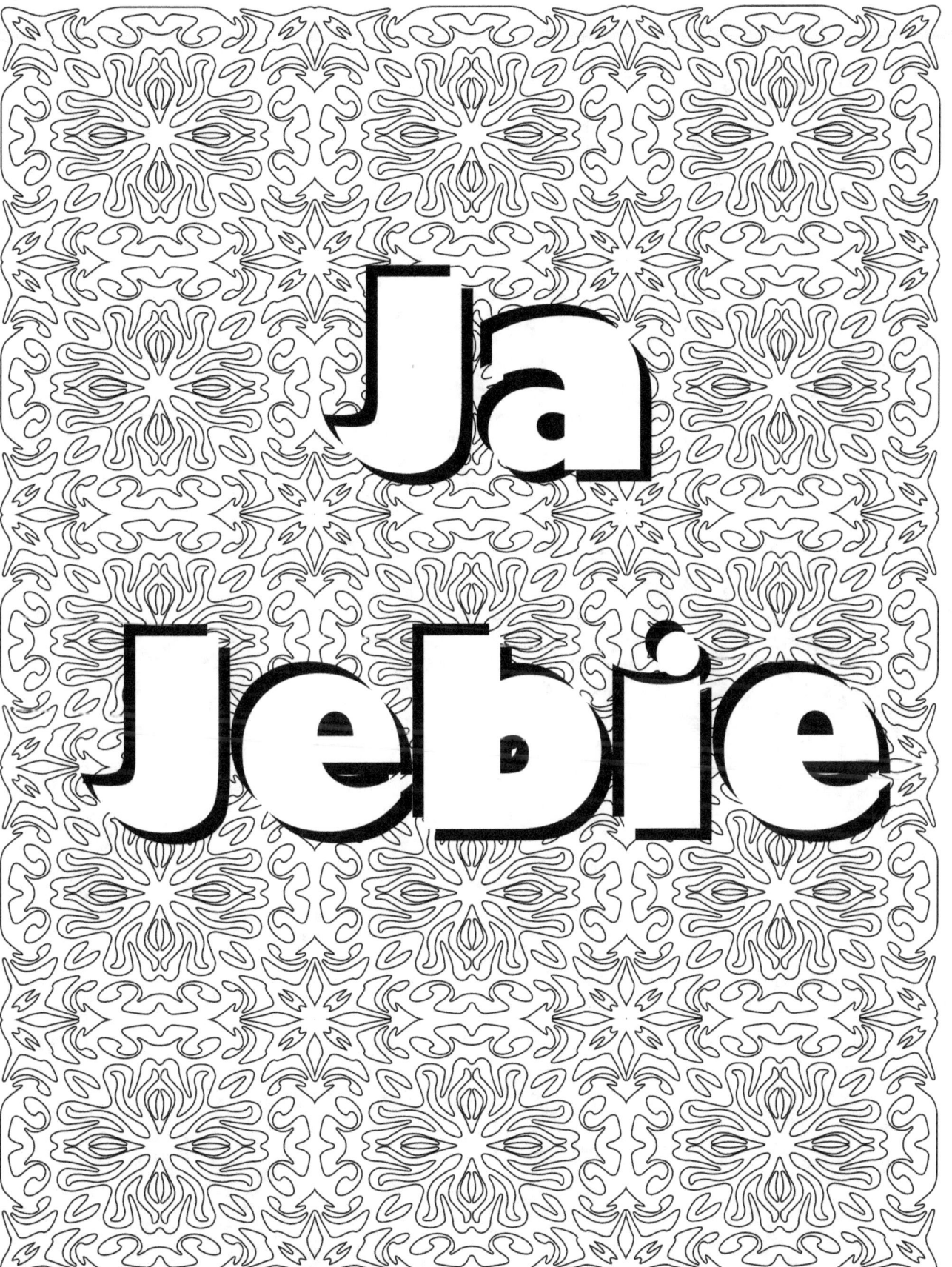

JESTEŚ

TOTALNA

ZDZIRA

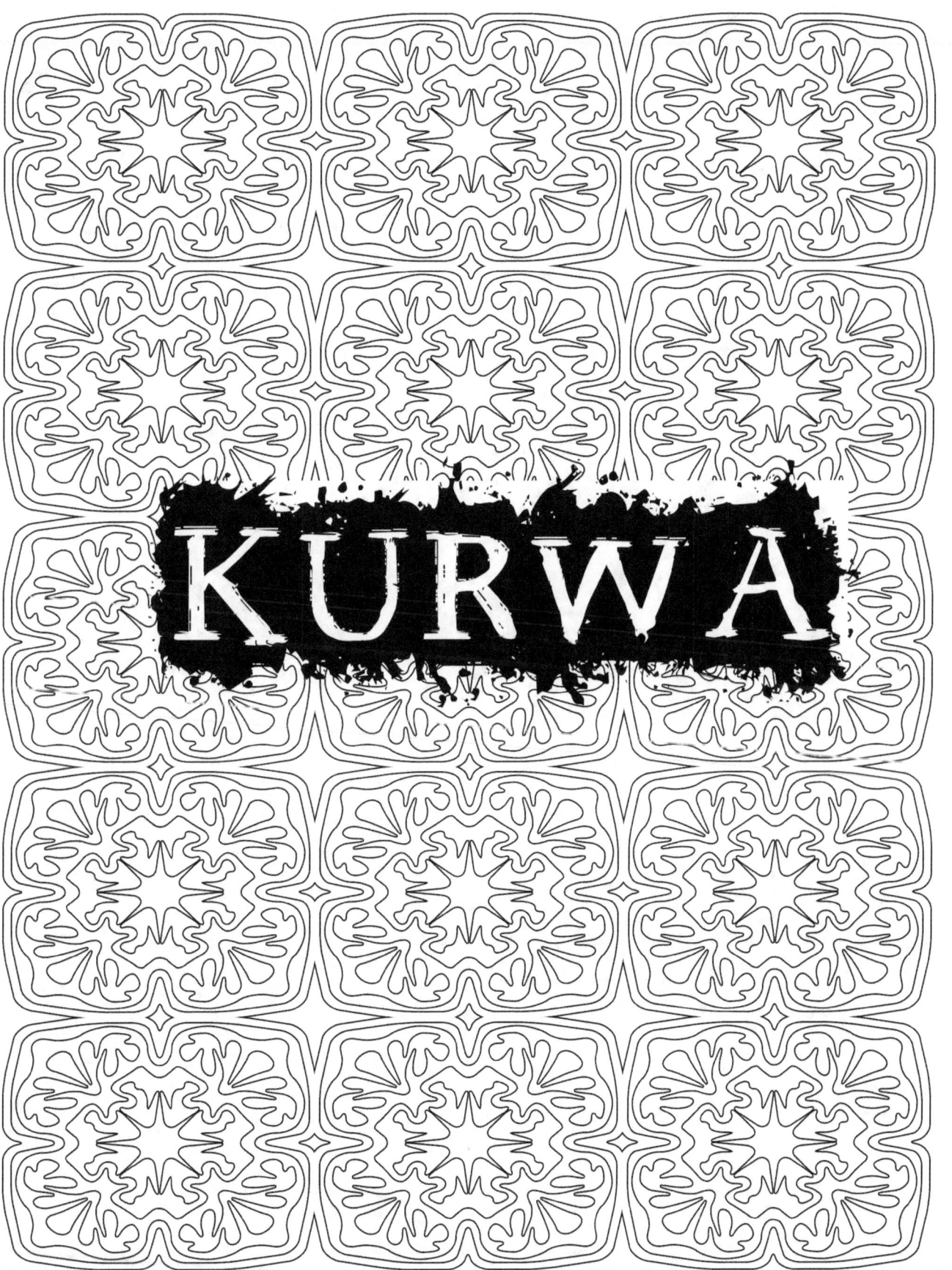

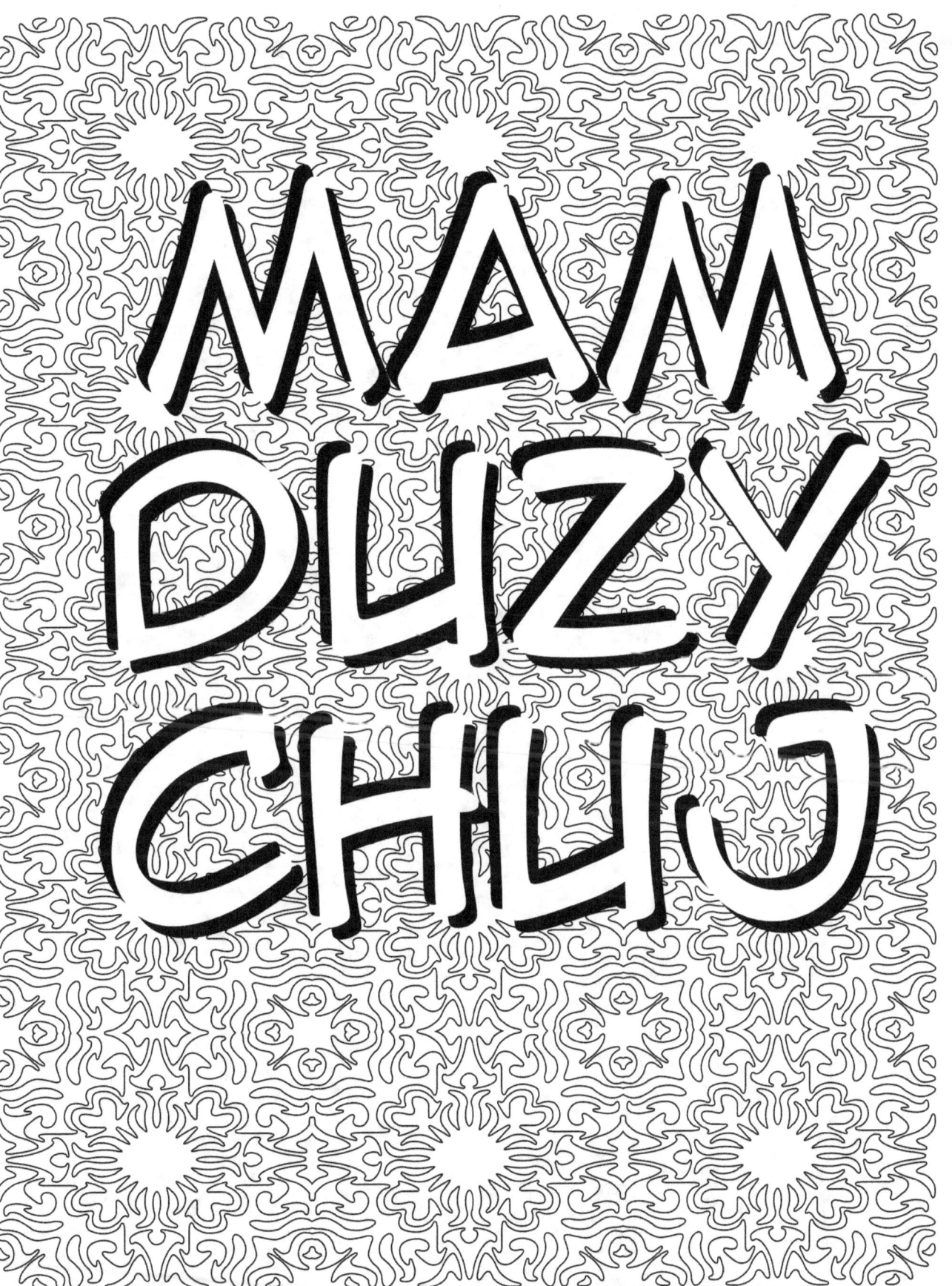

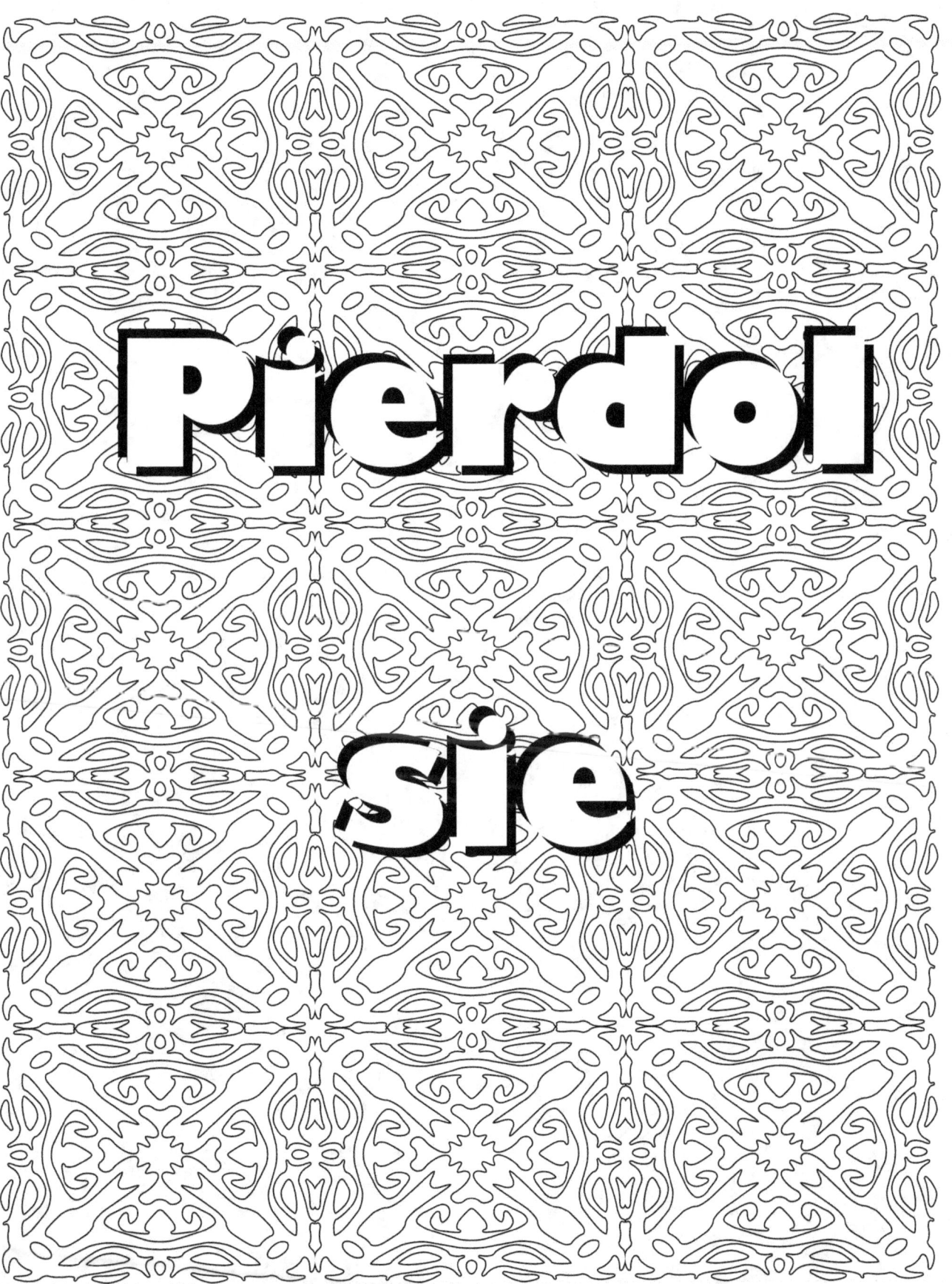

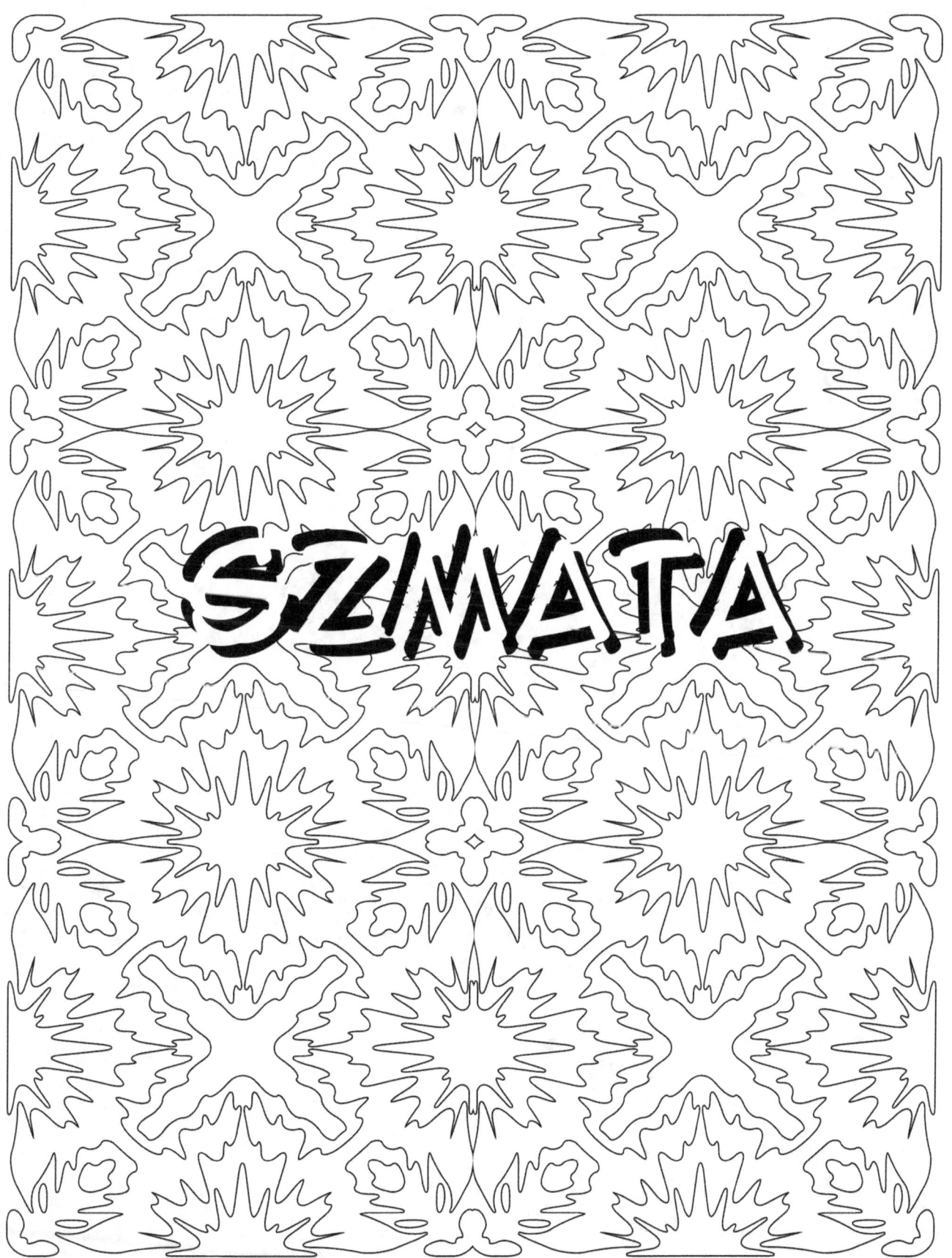

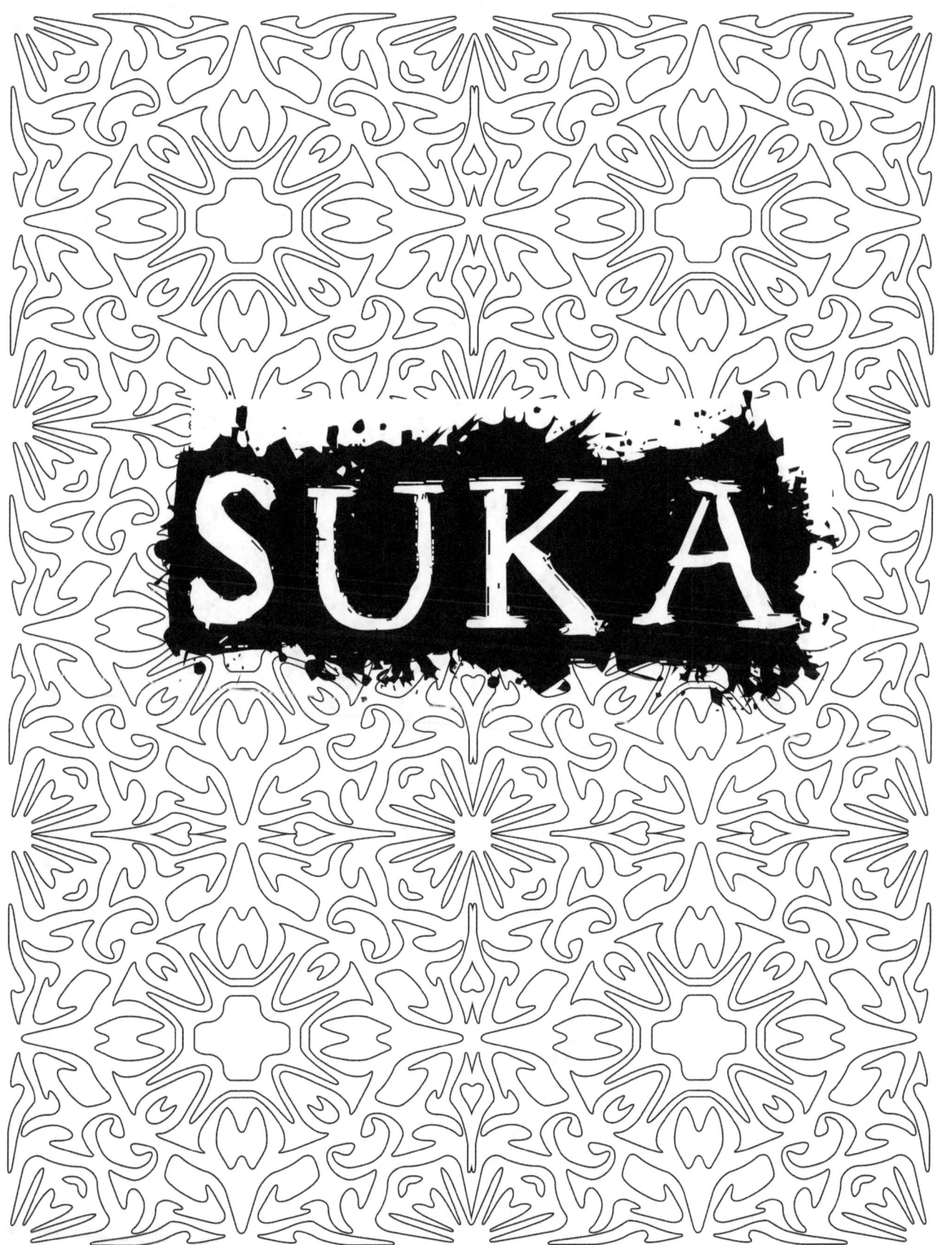

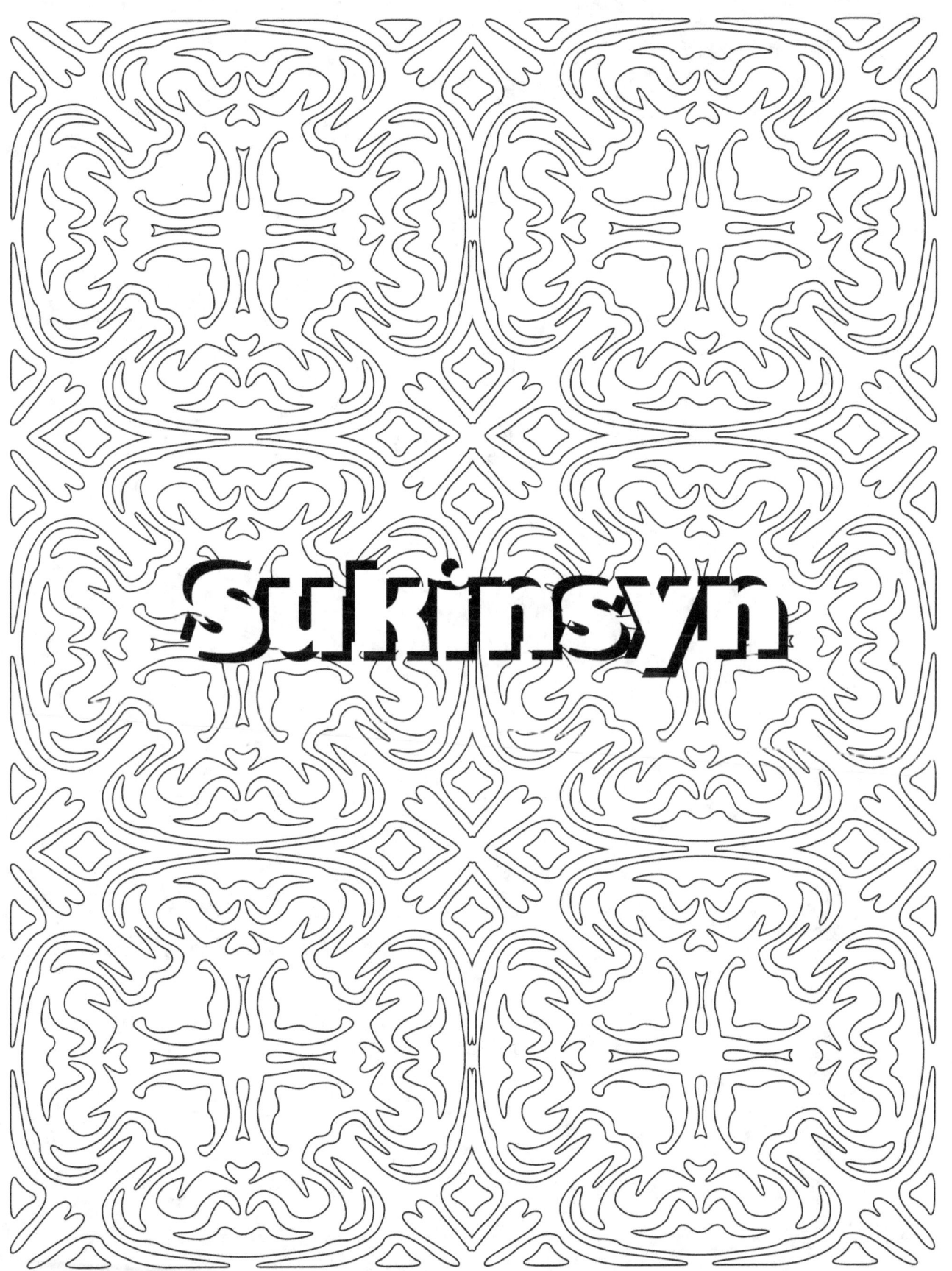

Sukinsyn

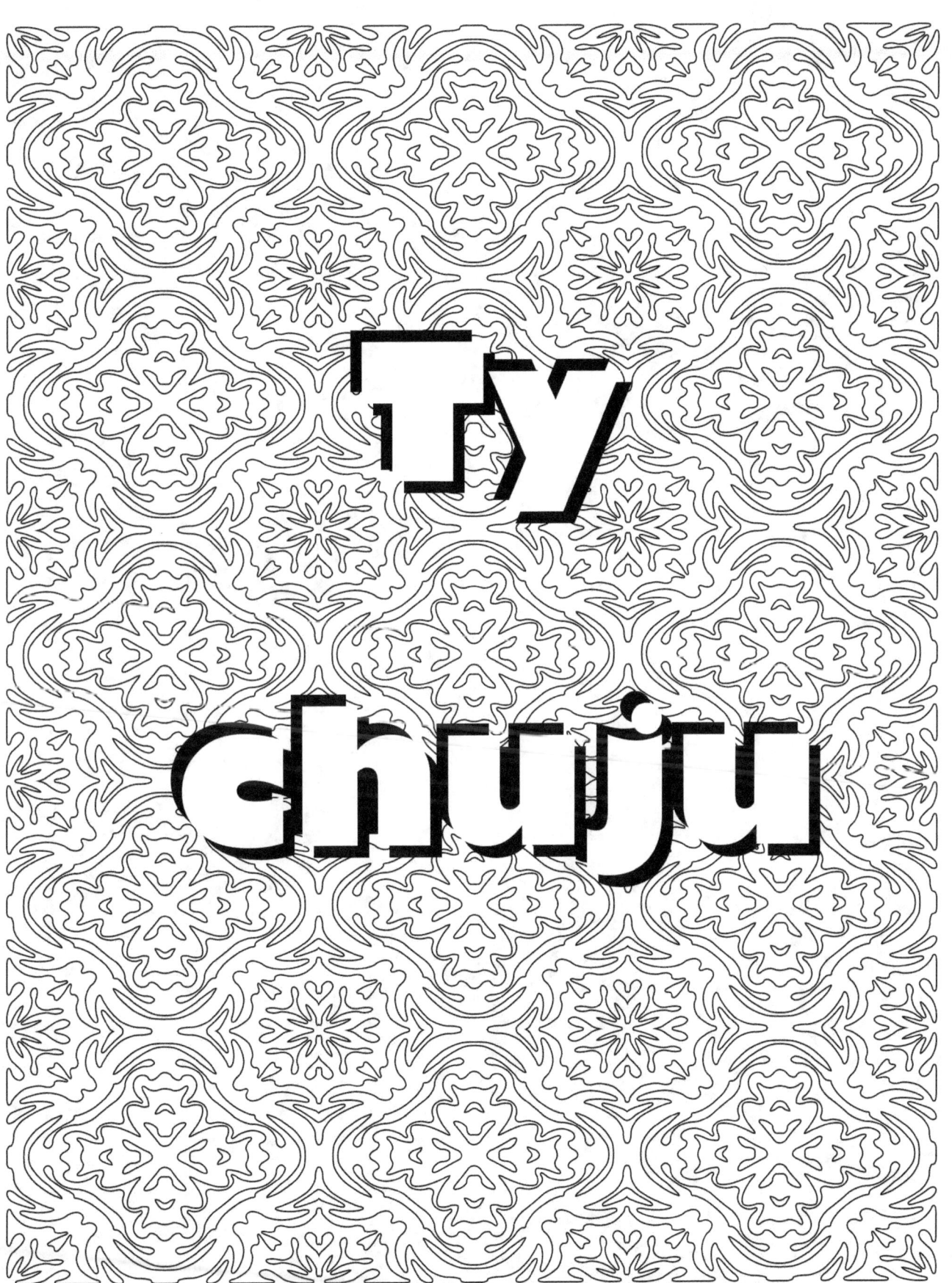

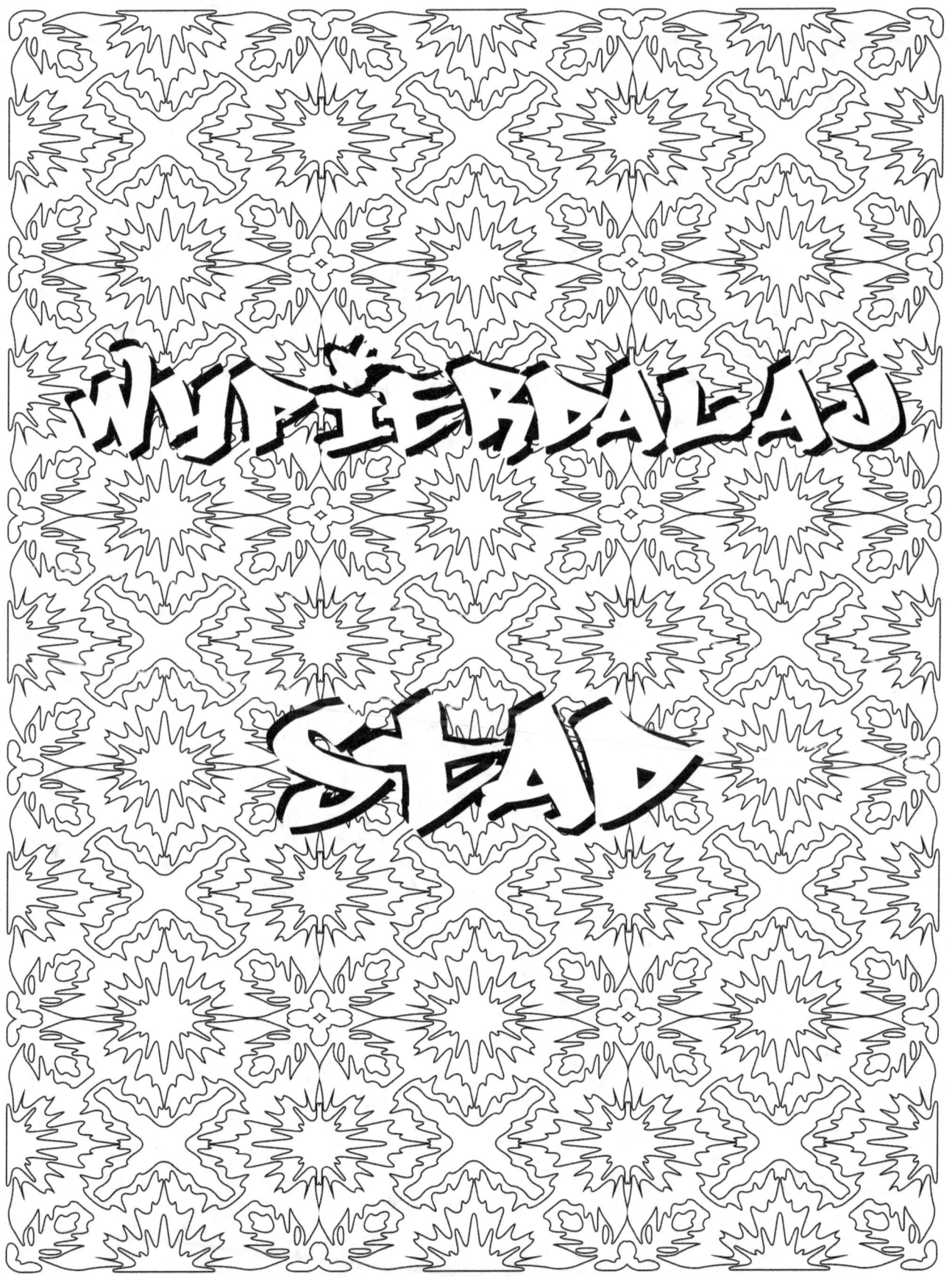

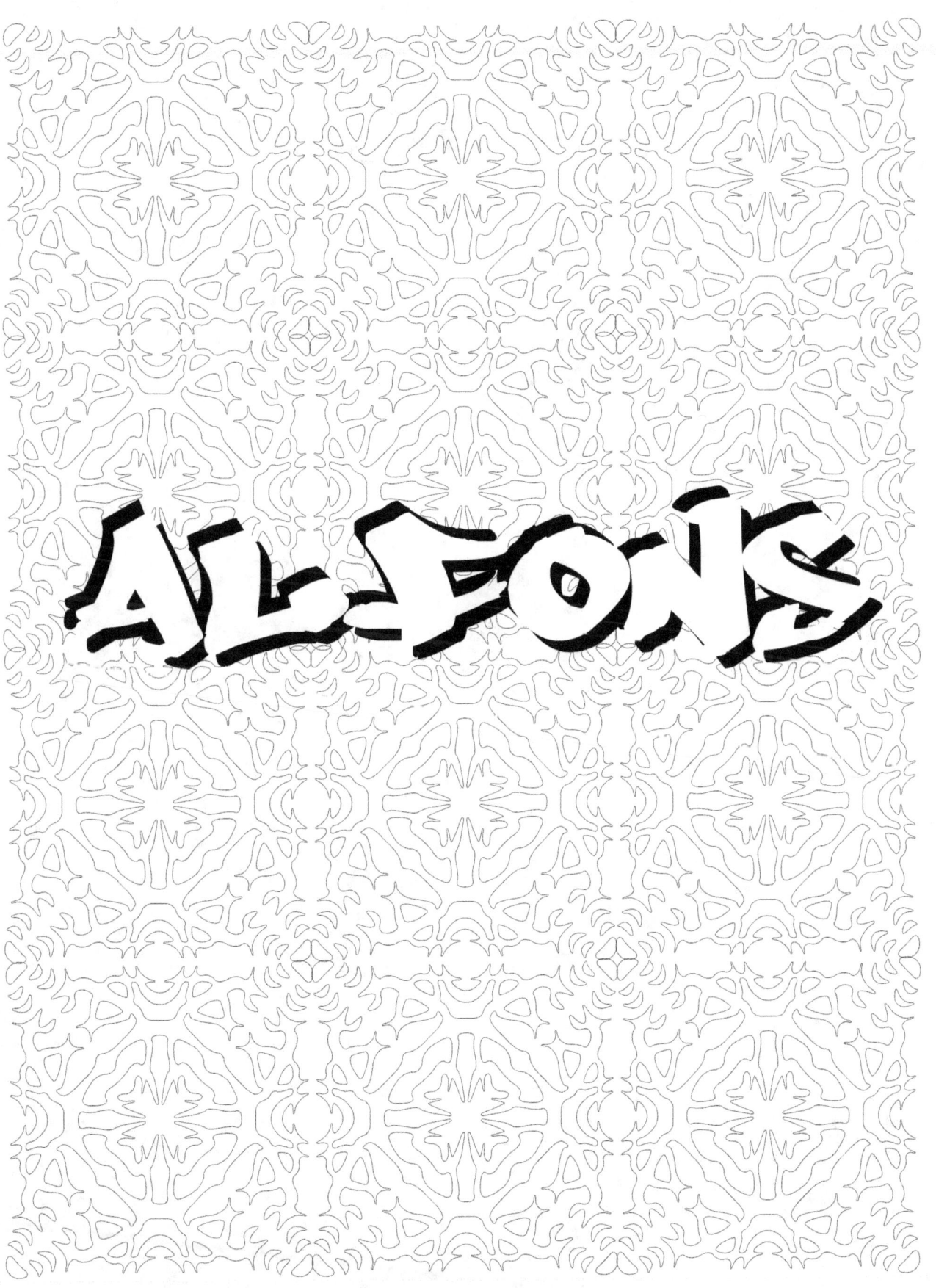

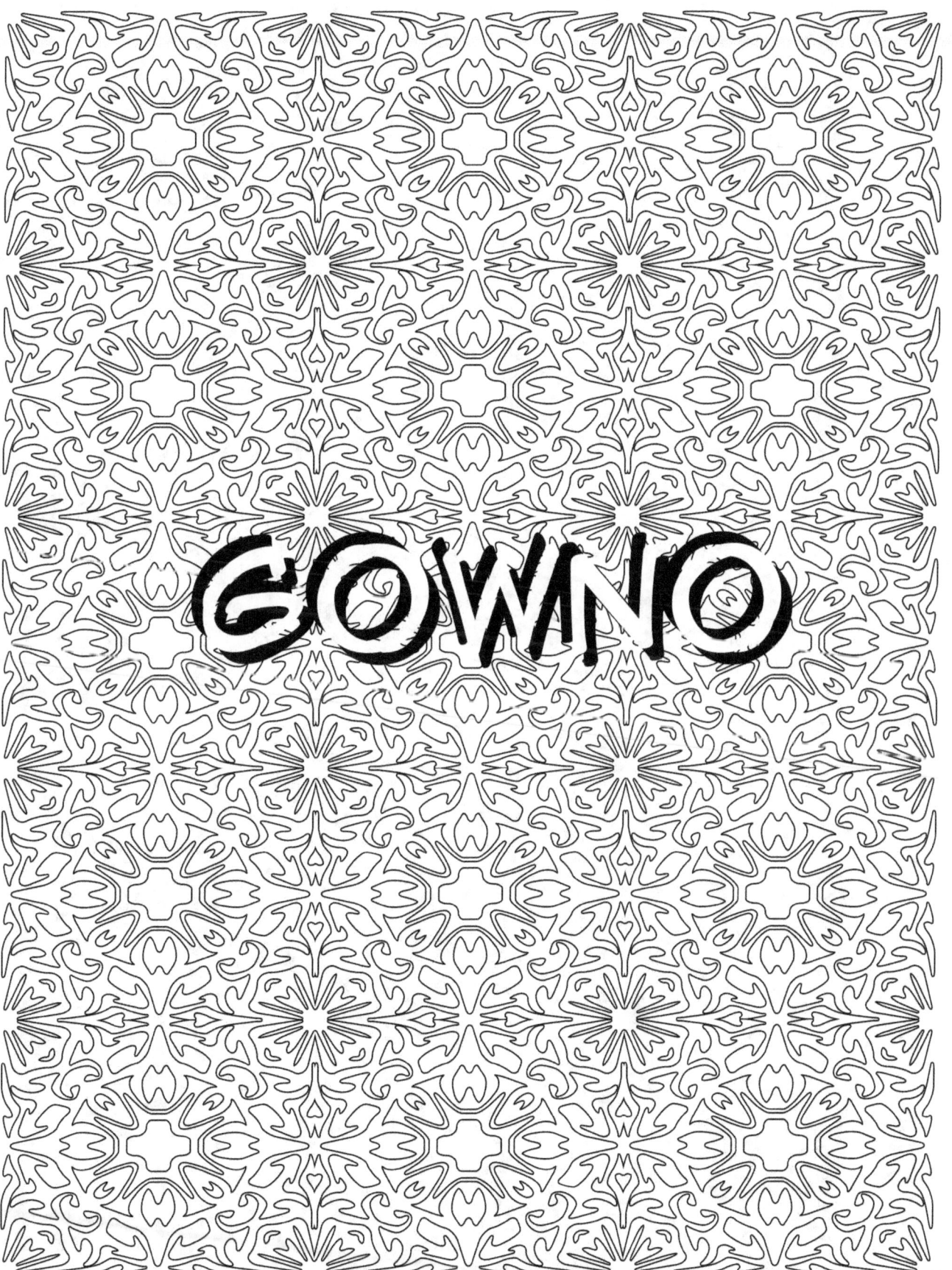

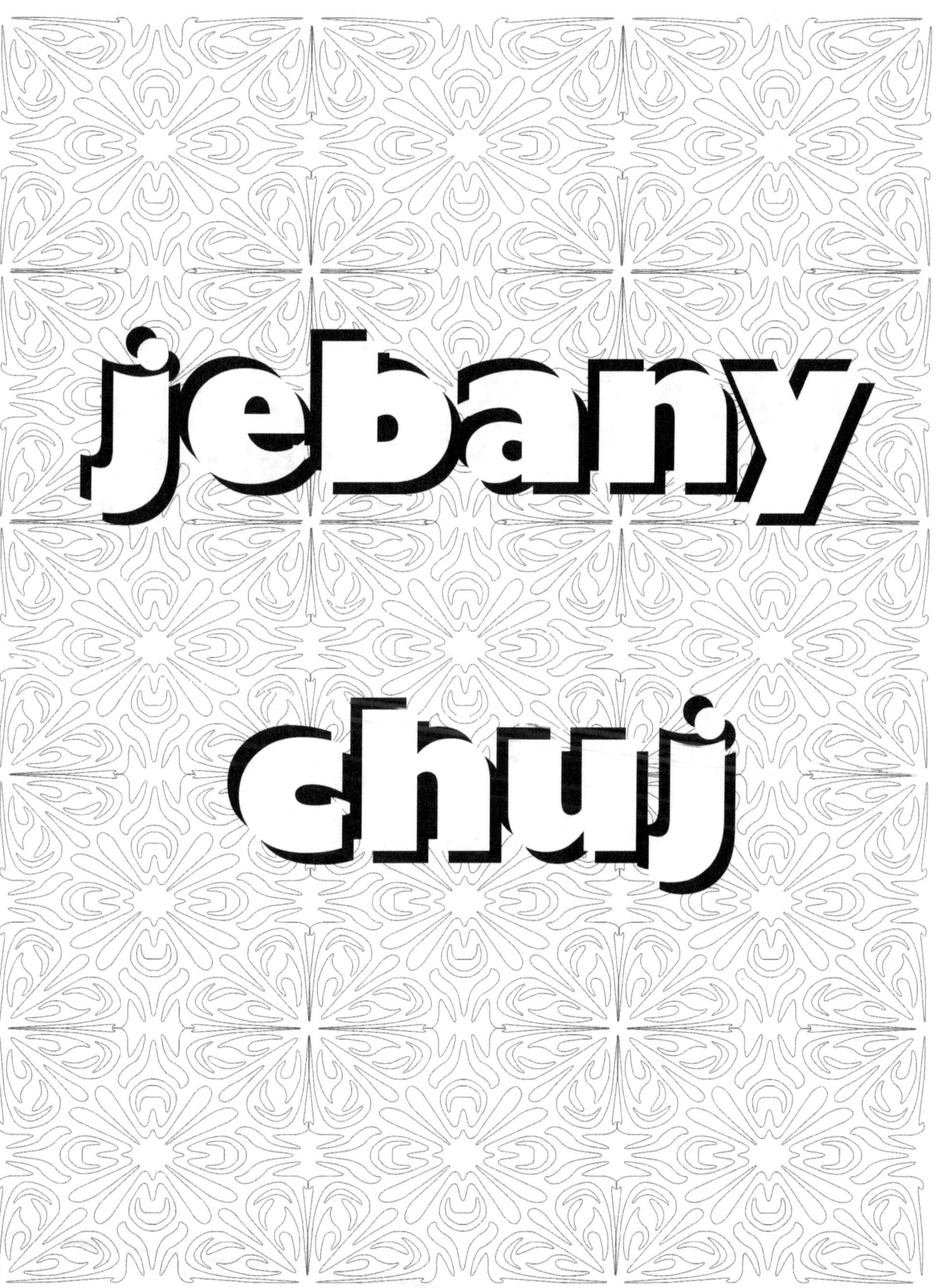

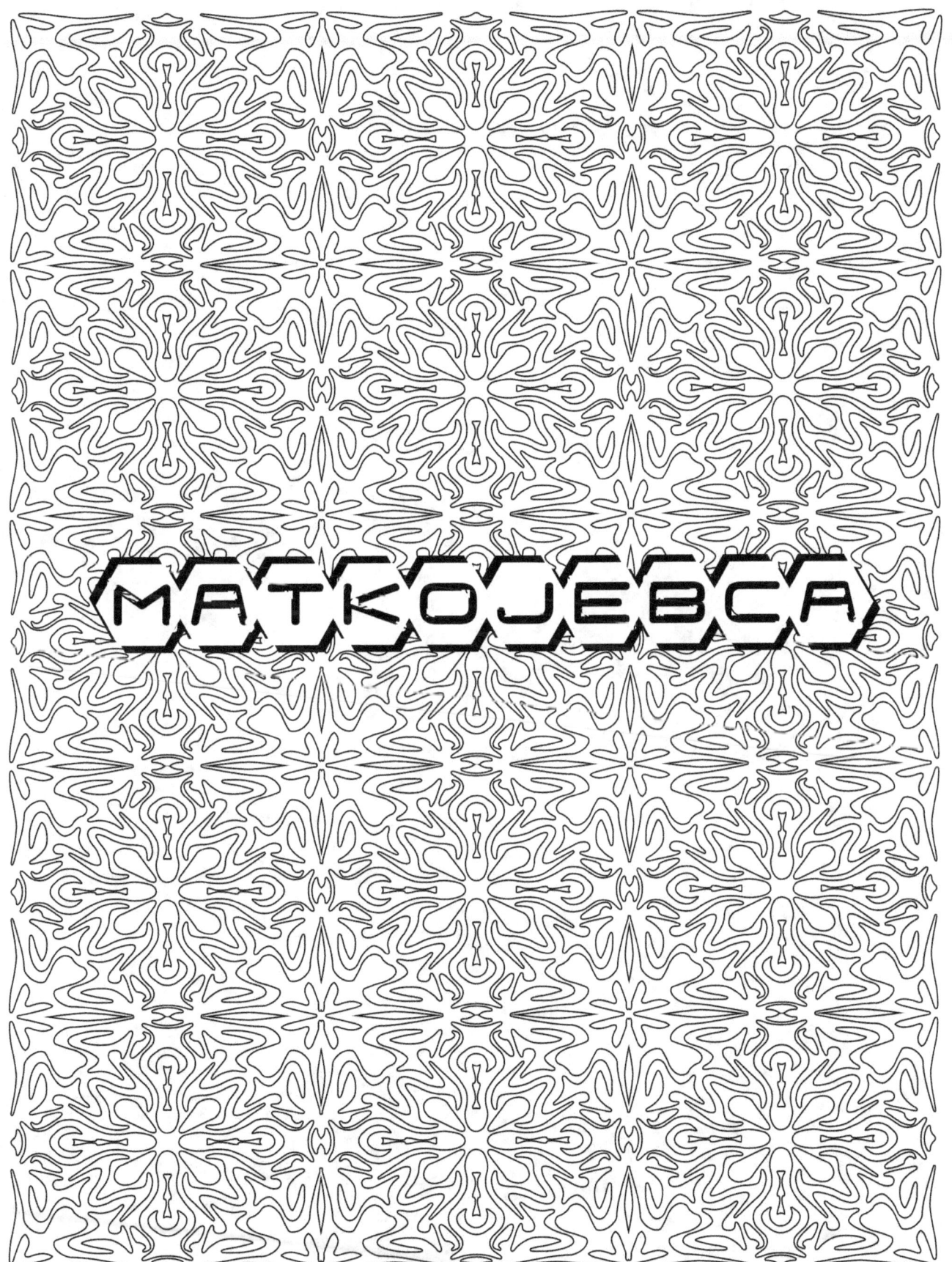

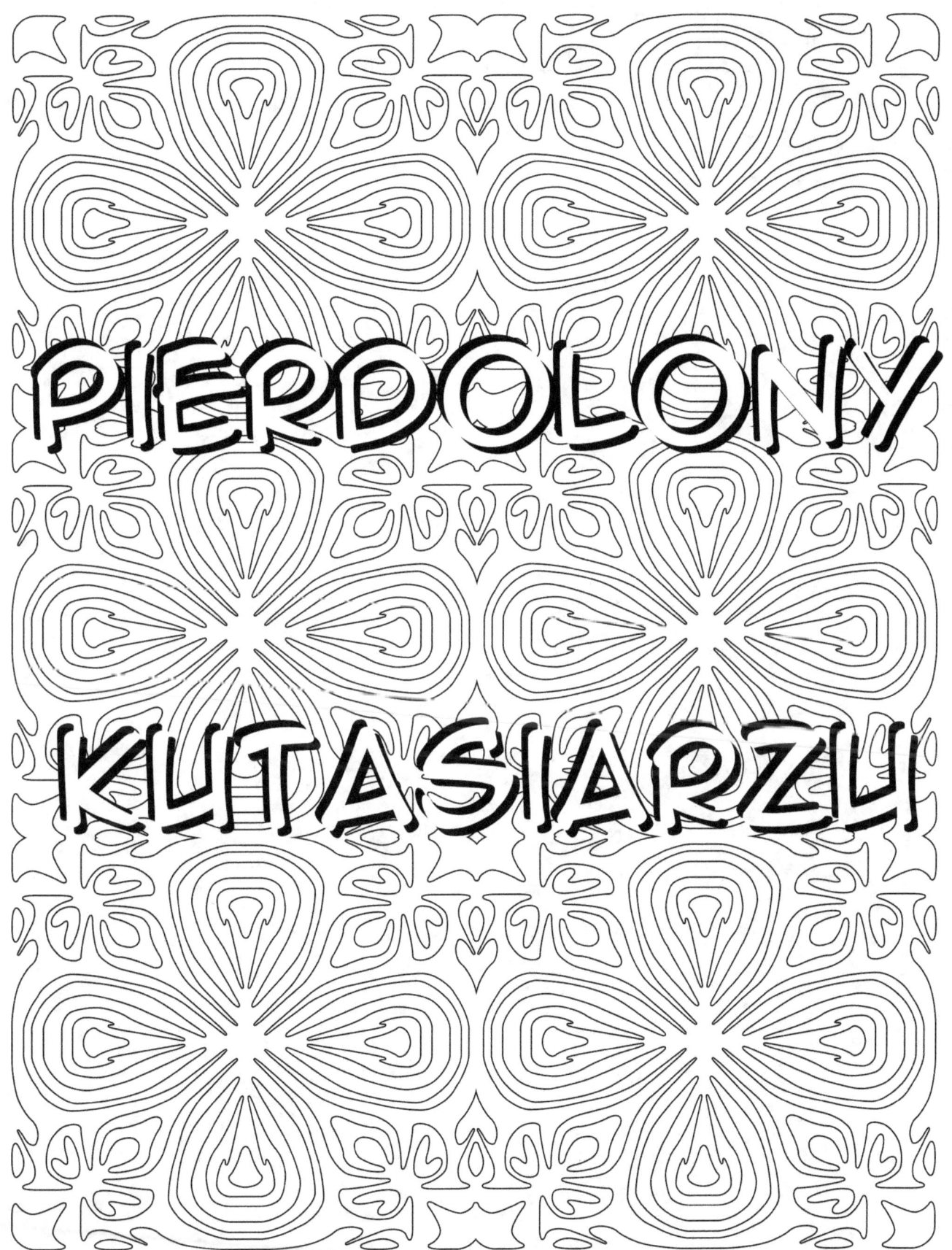

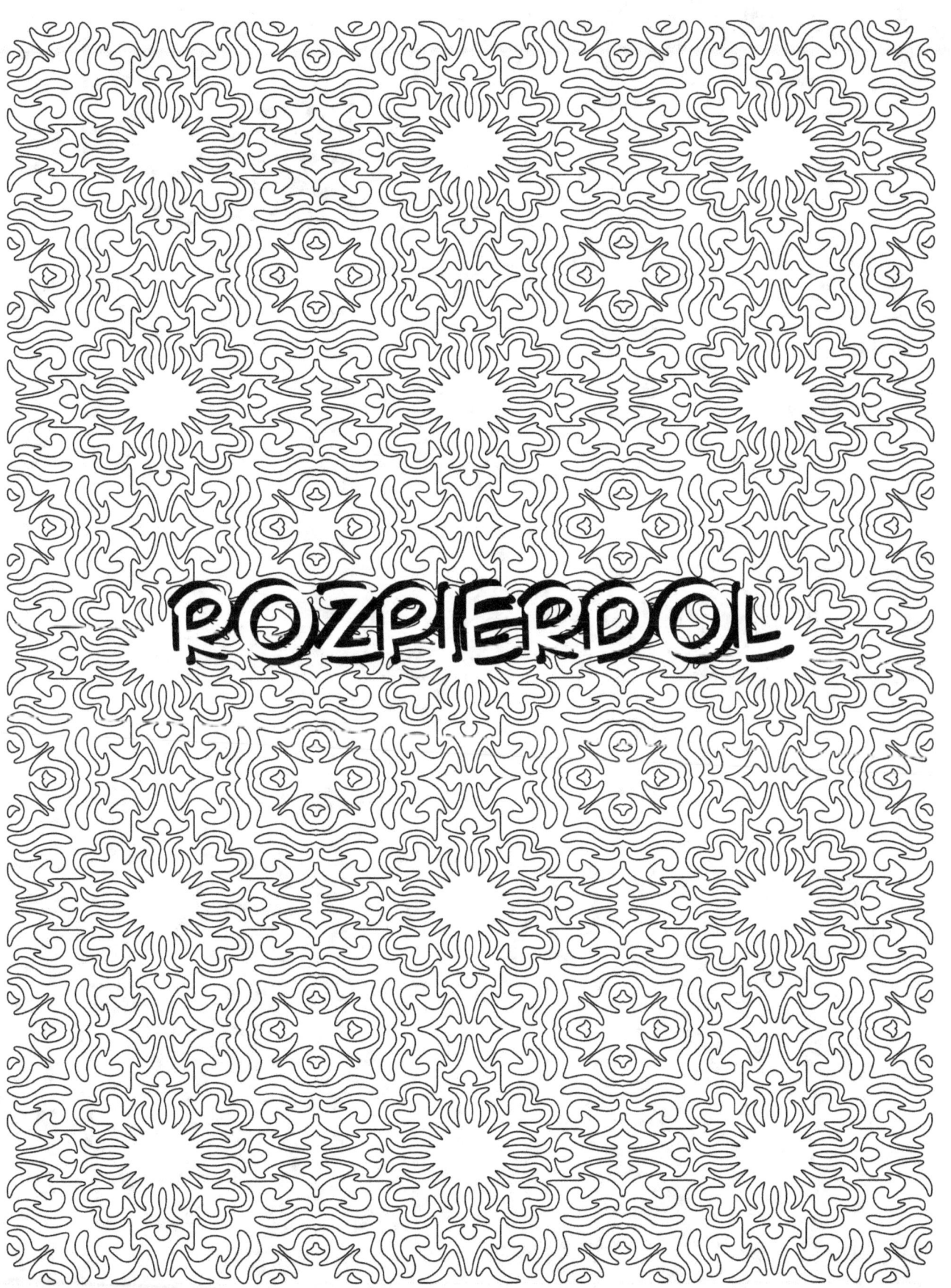

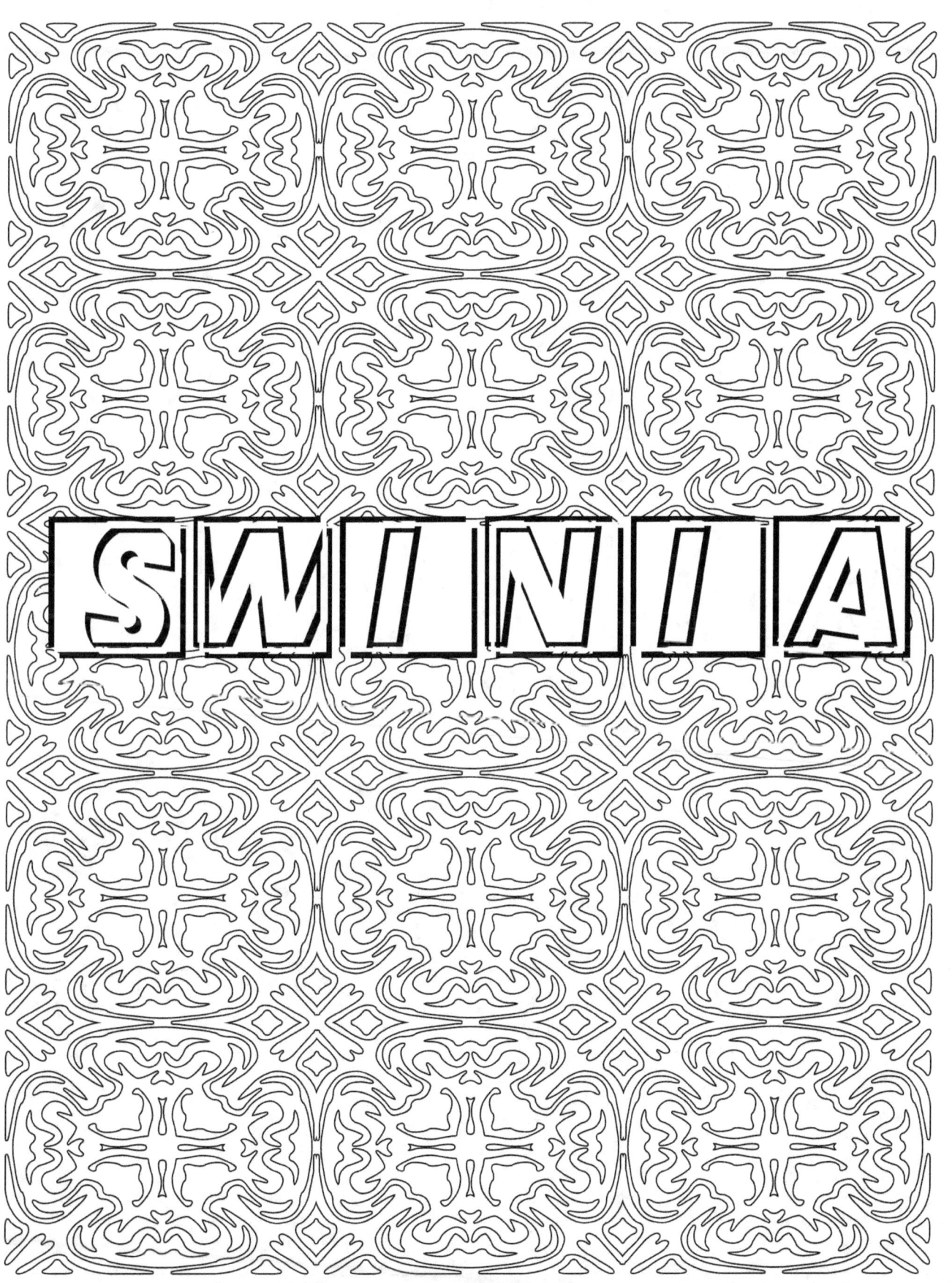

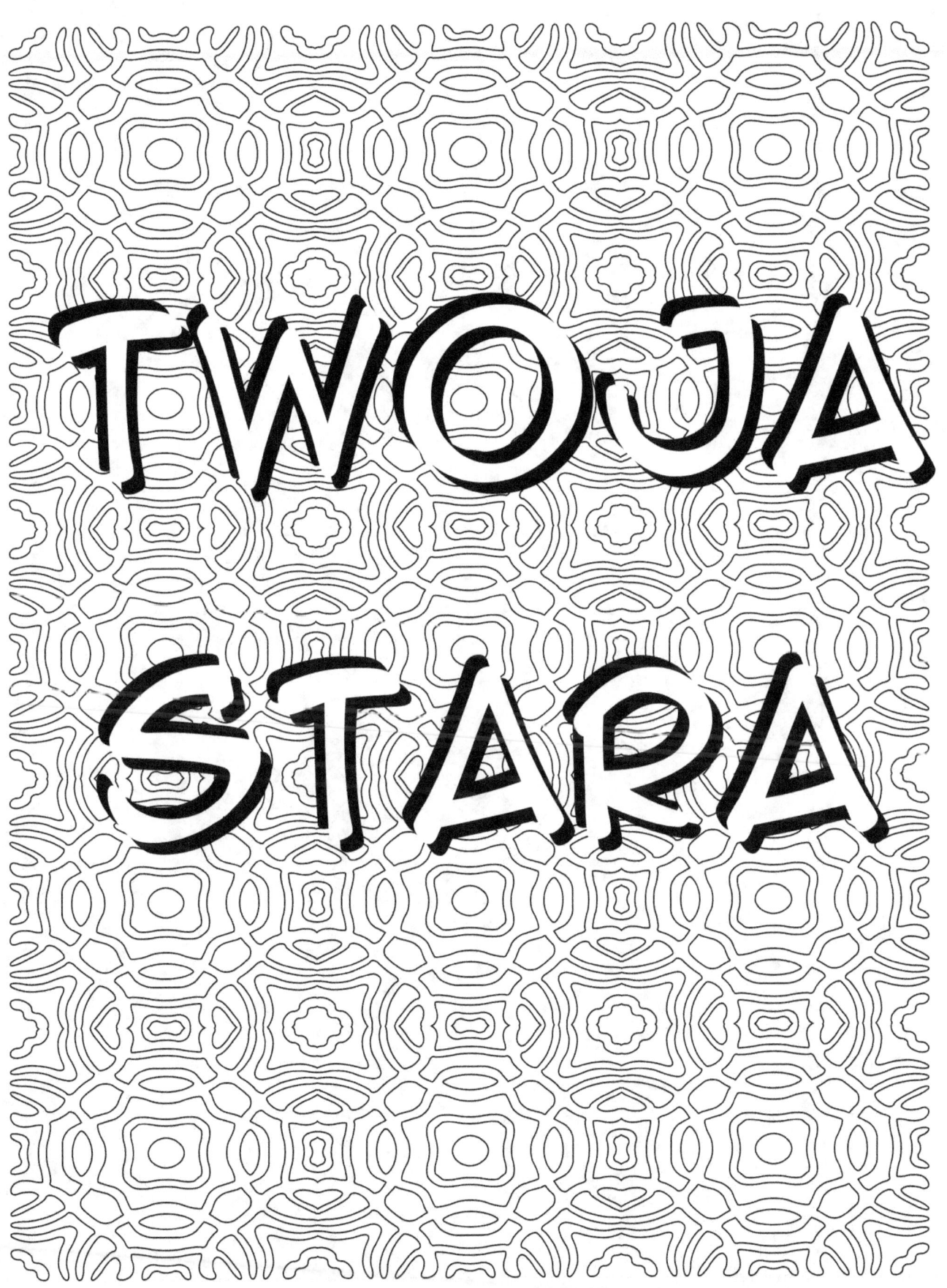

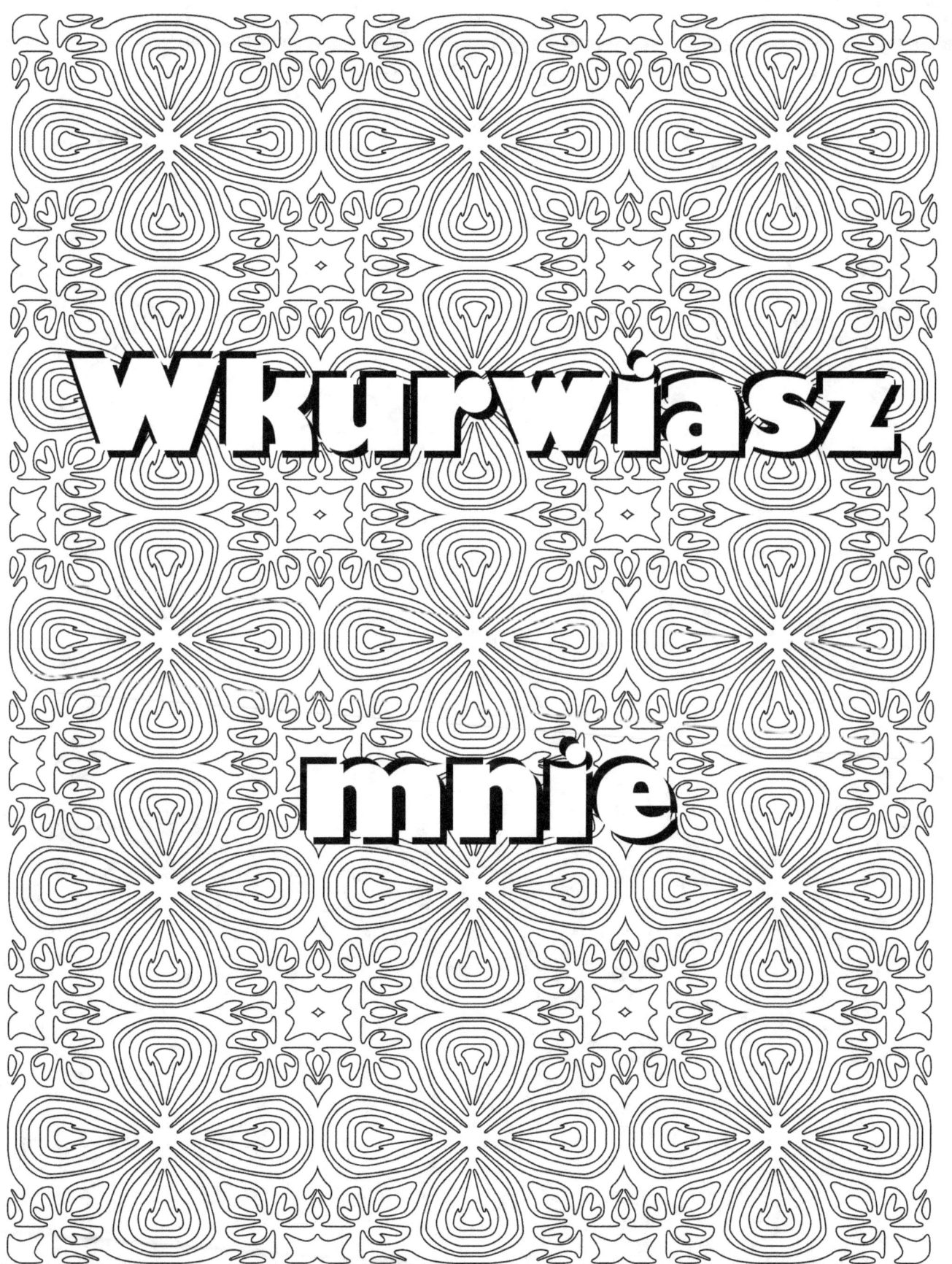

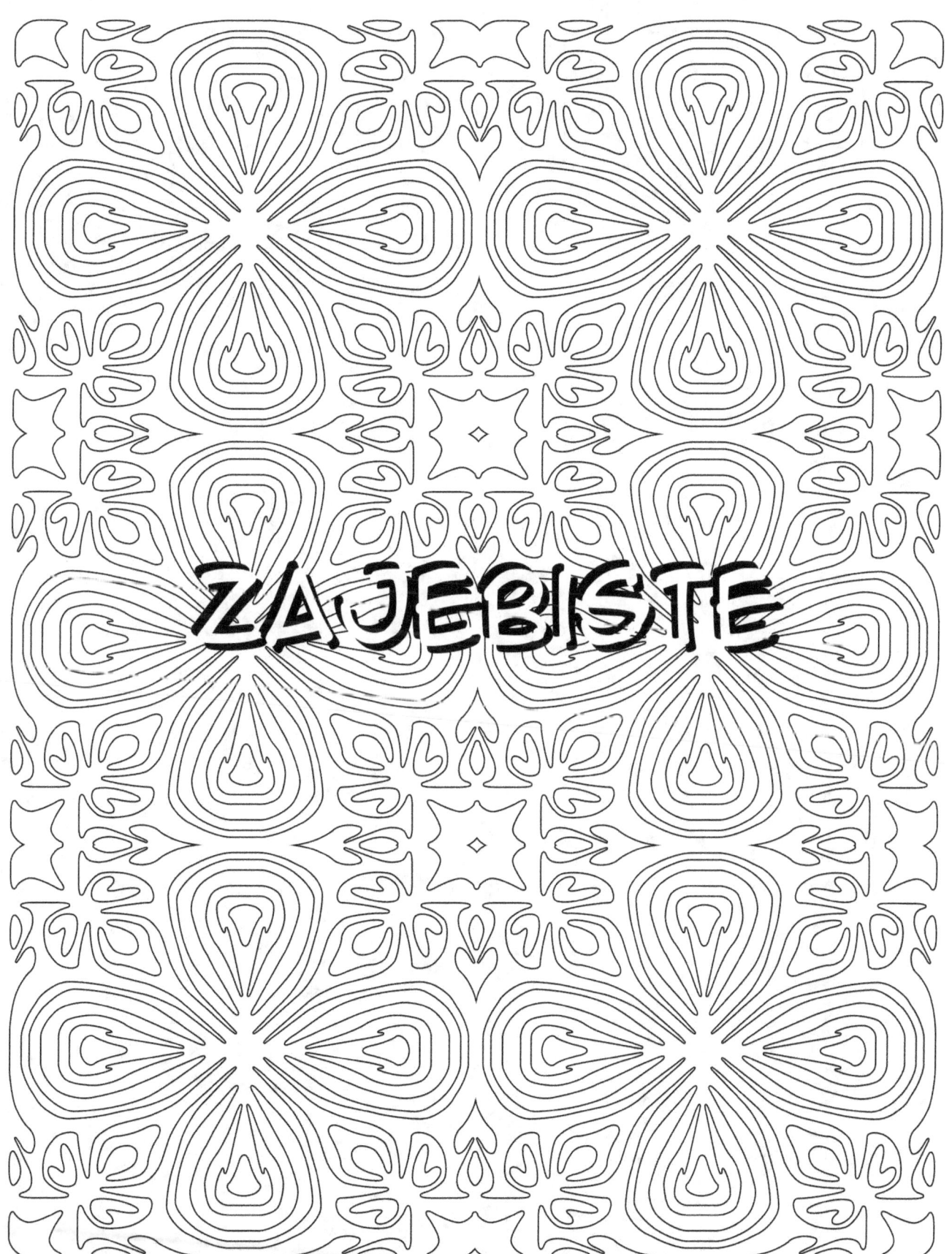

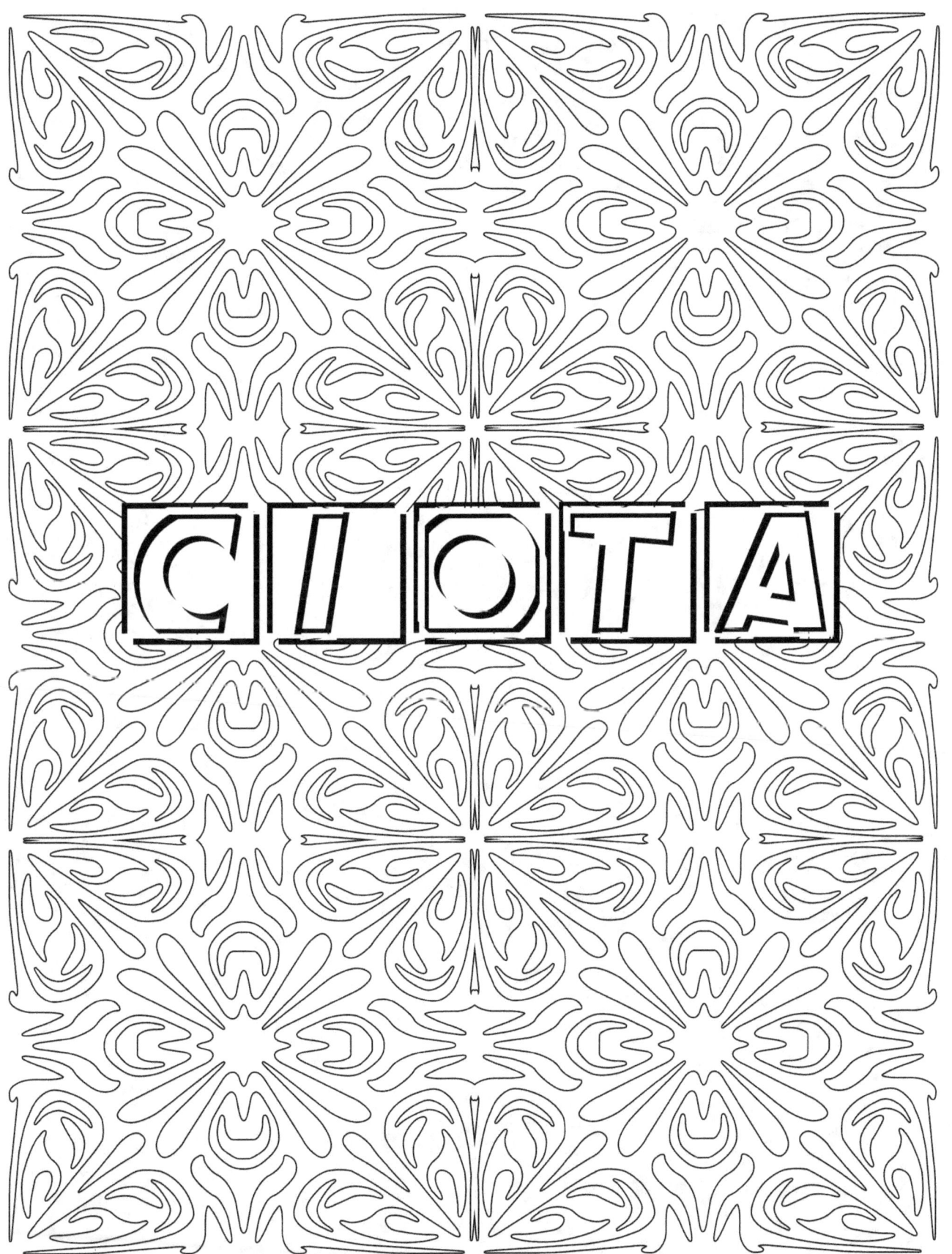

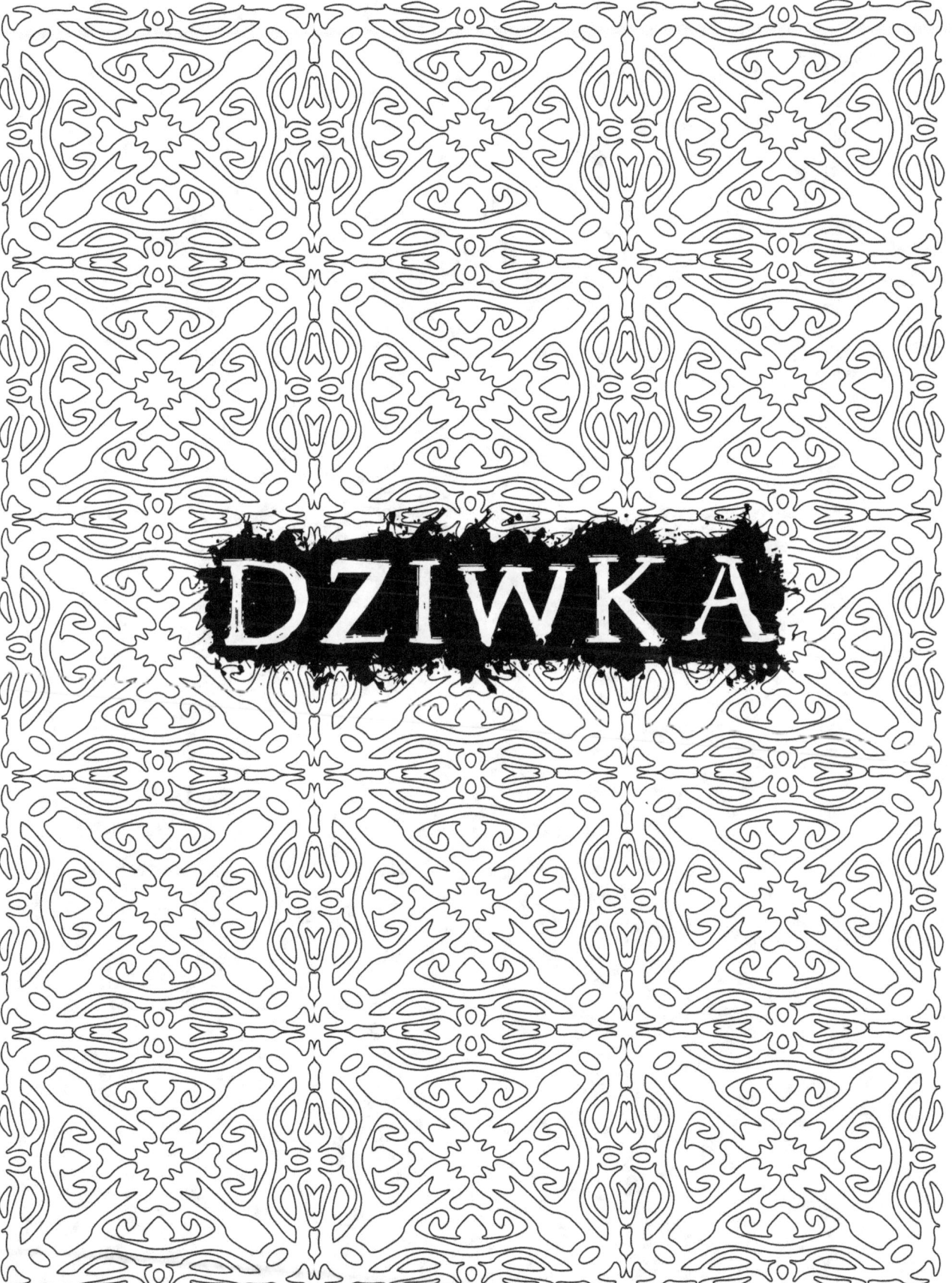

DZIWKA

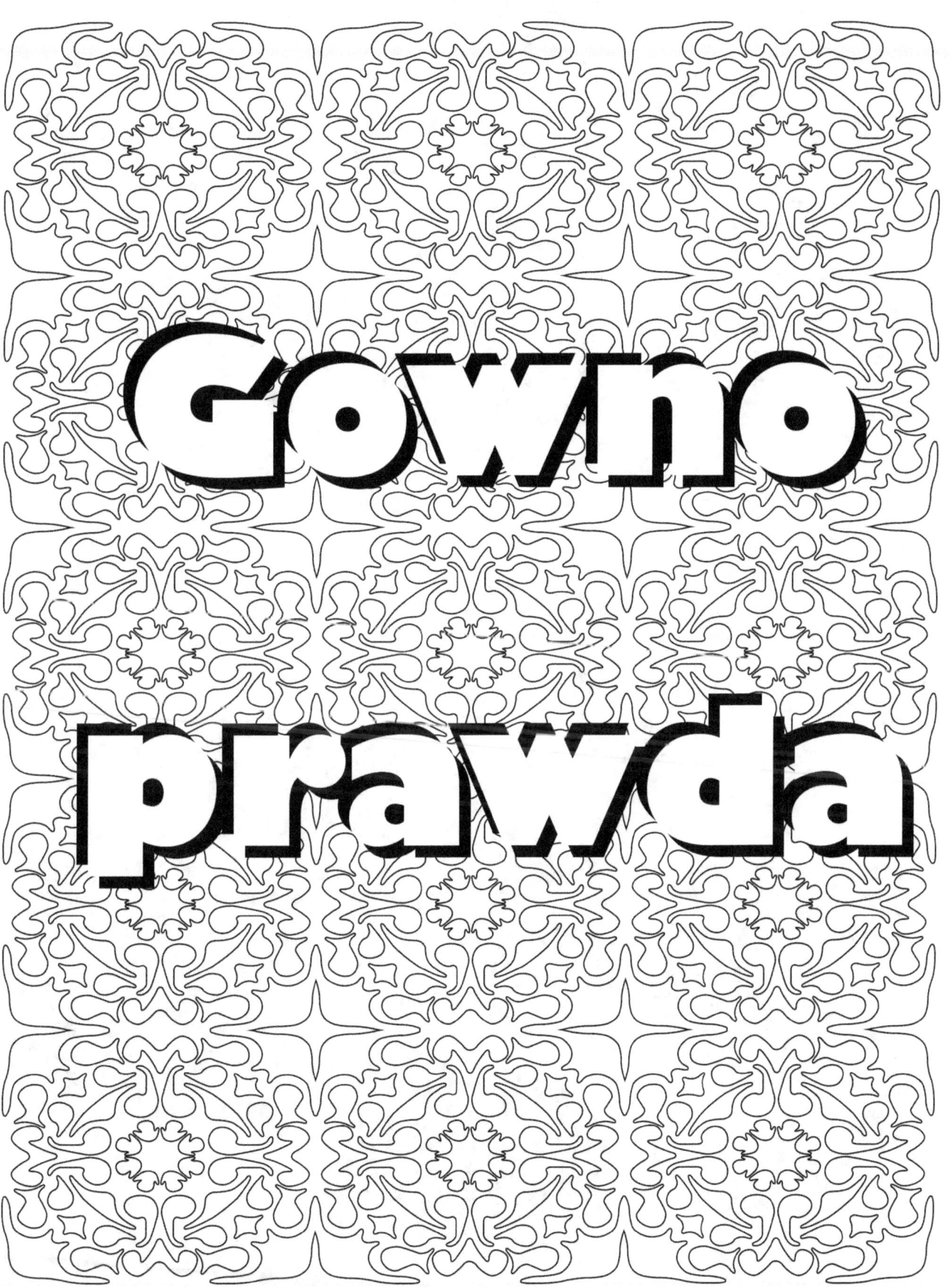

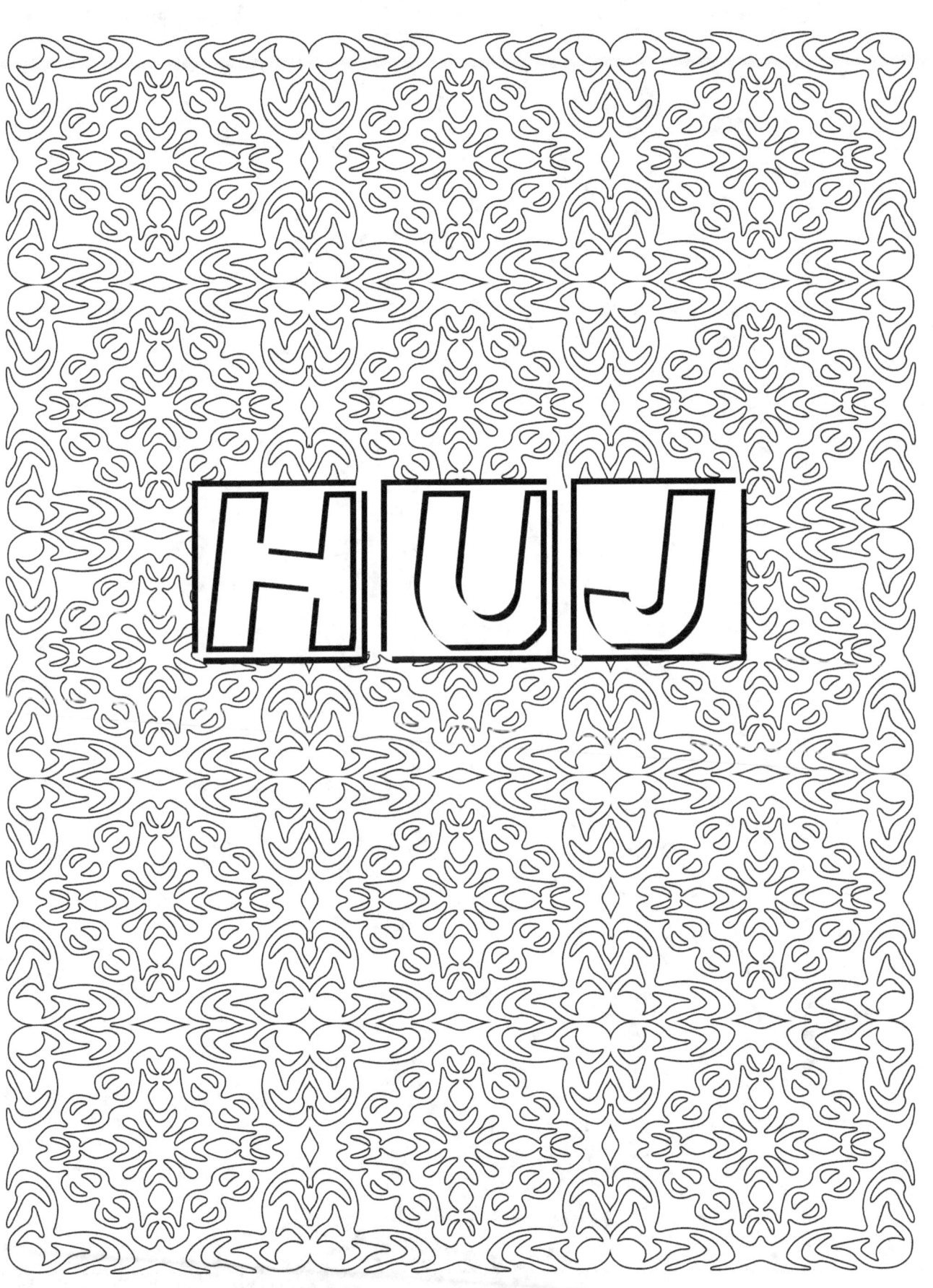

SZMATA

NIE

UMYTA

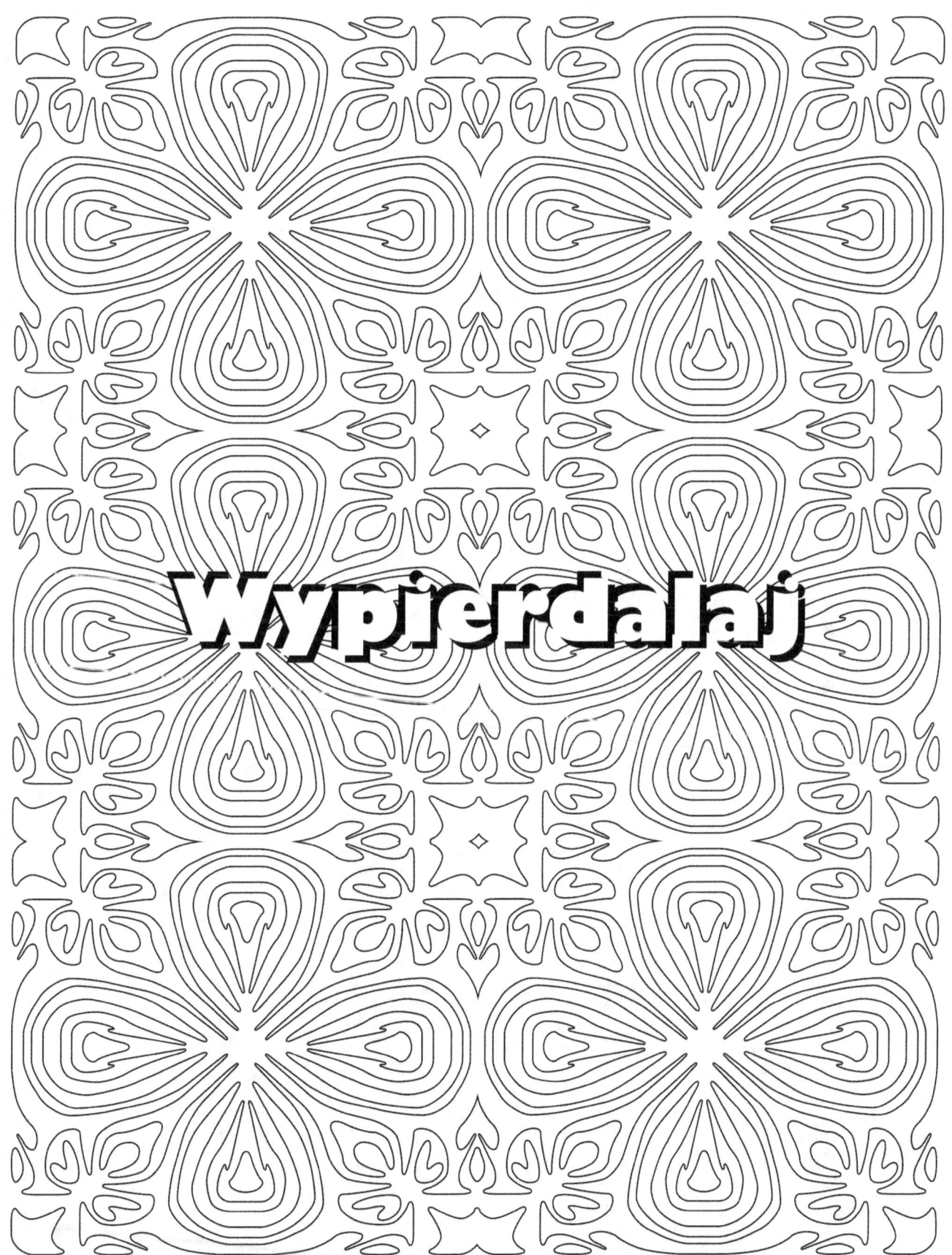

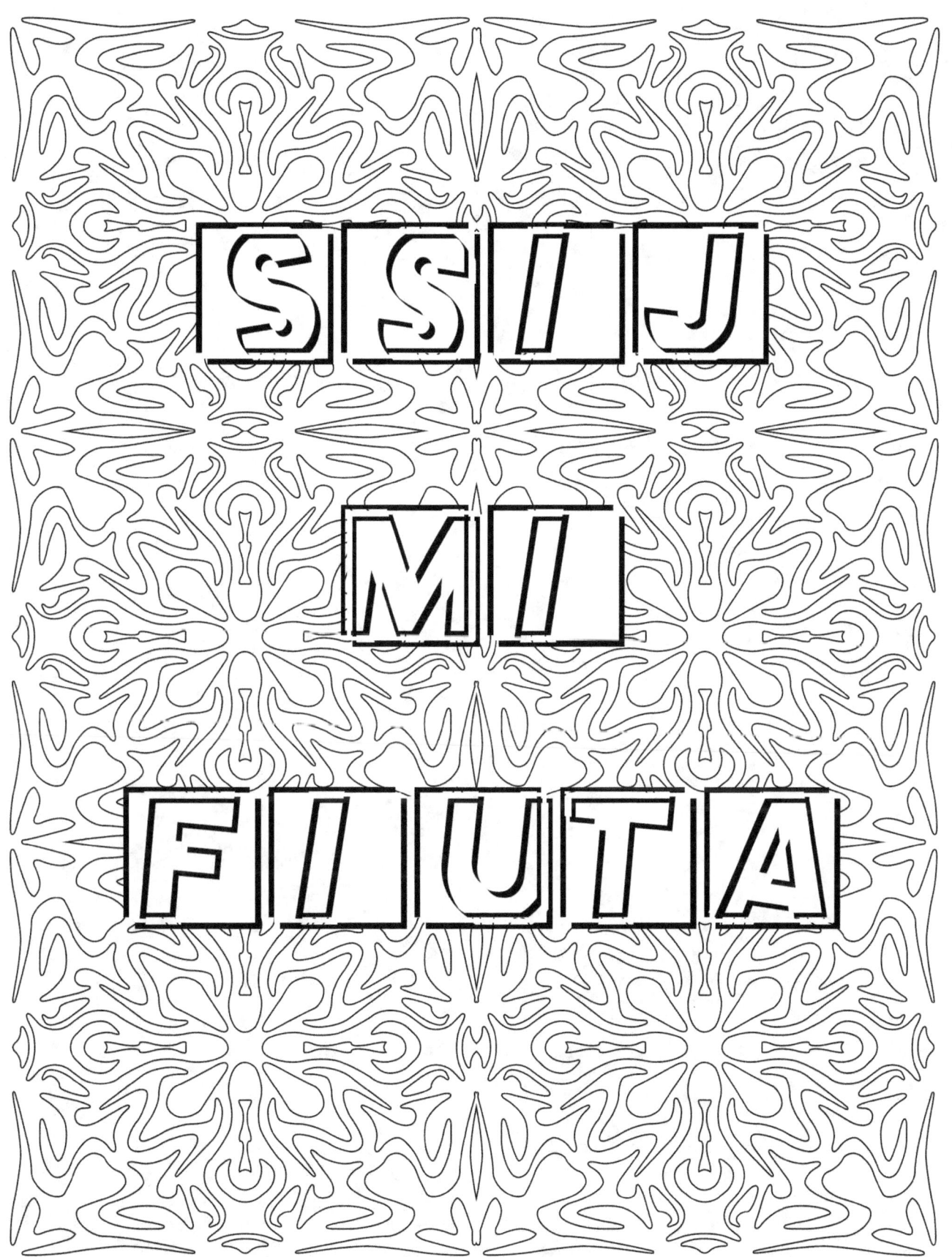

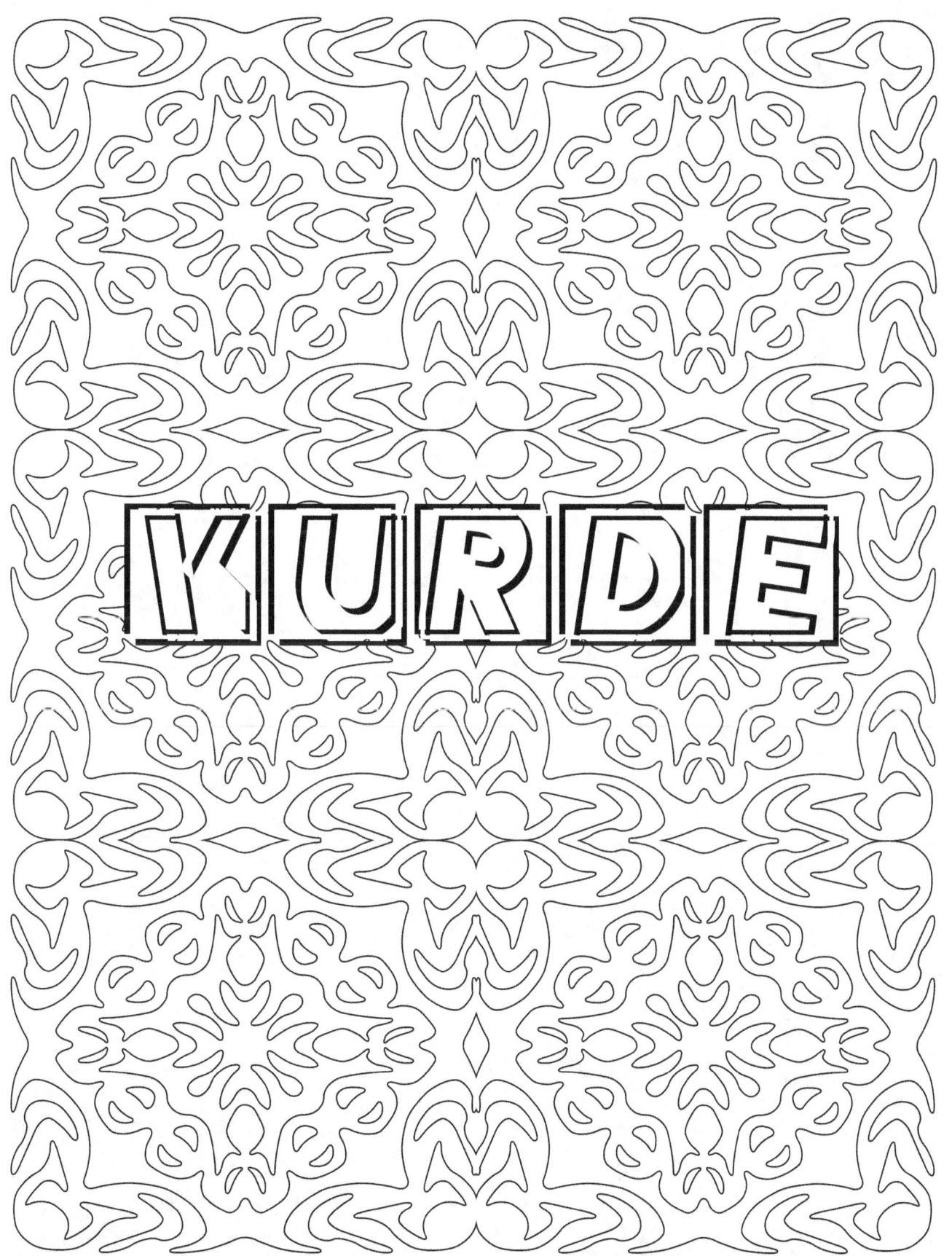

Final Words

Now Go Out There And Start Using Those Words!

Have Fun!

www.ingramcontent.com/pod-product-compliance
Lightning Source LLC
Chambersburg PA
CBHW081749220526
45468CB00008B/2303